Lee's Old War Horse: The Life and Career of General James Longstreet

By Charles River Editors

About Charles River Editors

Introduction

James Longstreet (1821–1904)

One of the most important, and controversial, Confederate generals during the Civil War was Lieutenant General James Longstreet, the man Robert E. Lee called his "old war horse." Longstreet was Lee's principal subordinate for most of the war, ably managing a corps in the Army of Northern Virginia and being instrumental in Confederate victories at Second Bull Run, Fredericksburg, and Chickamauga. Longstreet was also effective at Antietam and the Battle of the Wilderness, where he was nearly killed by a shot through the neck.

Had Longstreet died on the field in early May 1864, he would almost certainly be considered one of the South's biggest heroes. However, it was his performance at Gettysburg and arguments with other Southern generals after the Civil War that tarnished his image. After the South lost the war and Gettysburg came to be viewed as one of its biggest turning points, former Confederate generals looked to that battle to find scapegoats to blame for losing the war. Longstreet was charged with being slow to attack on the second day of the Battle of Gettysburg, allowing the Union to man Little Round Top. He also resisted Lee's order for Pickett's Charge the next day, making his criticisms clear both that day and after the war through his rightings. The fact that he served in Republican administrations after the Civil War rubbed his former comrades the wrong way, and the Georgian Longstreet's criticism of Lee infuriated the Virginian Lost Cause advocates who idolized Lee.

Near the end of his life, Longstreet authored *From Manassas to Appomattox*, a Civil War memoirs that looked to rebut his critics. Longstreet didn't avoid his critics, facing them head on by fending off criticisms of his record for the most part, usually including letters written by other officers to his defense. Longstreet also didn't pull punches, which he does at times quite poignantly on Lee's mishaps, most notably of course at Gettysburg. In other instances, he defends himself by criticizing others. When Fitz Lee notes that R.E. Lee called Longstreet the hardest man to move in the Army (a comment that can't be confirmed or refuted), he comes to his own defense in part by criticizing Stonewall Jackson during the Seven Days campaign. Hindsight is 20/20, and Longstreet's arguments in the conduct of certain campaigns certainly benefited from the passing of 30 years. At a number of places, Longstreet believes that if his suggestions were followed, the results could have destroyed Union armies or won the War. Nobody will ever be sure if he's right or wrong on these matters, though historians typically consider those kinds of statements bluster.

Lee's Old Warhorse: The Life and Career of General James Longstreet looks at the life and career of one of the South's most important and controversial fighters, explaining his biggest accomplishments and discussing the biggest controversies. Along with pictures of Longstreet and other important people, places and events in his life, you will learn about Lee's Old War Horse like you never have before, in no time at all.

Chapter 1: Family Lineage

The Longstreet Family Tree

James (K.*) Longstreet was born on January 8, 1821 in Edgefield District, South Carolina (now part of North Augusta, Edgefield County), the fifth child and third son to James Longstreet (1783-1833) and Mary Ann Dent (1793-1855). Originally from New Jersey and Maryland respectively, the senior James owned a cotton plantation near the modern city of Gainesville in northeastern Georgia. James' ancestor, Dirck Stoffels Langestraet, immigrated to the Dutch colony of New Netherlands in 1657, with the "Longstreet" name becoming Anglicized over the generations.

*(All formal documents available list James Longstreet as his full name, while several informal papers included the "K" initial but no clarification of what it stands for.)

According to Longstreet's memoirs, which are still widely considered one of the most important memoirs written about the Civil War: "Grandfather William Longstreet first applied steam as a motive power, in 1787, to a small boat on the Savannah River at Augusta, and spent all of his private means upon that idea, asked aid of his friends in Augusta and elsewhere, had no encouragement, but, on the contrary, ridicule of his proposition to move a boat without a pulling or other external power, and especially did they ridicule the thought of expensive steam-boilers to be made of iron. To obviate costly outlay for this item, he built boilers of heavy oak timbers and strong iron bands, but the Augusta marines were incredulous…"

Of course, history does not credit William Longstreet for the discovery. What happened? According to Longstreet, "He failed to secure the necessary aid, and the discovery passed into the possession of certain New Yorkers, who found the means for practicable application, and now steam is the goddess that enlightens the world."

Chapter 2: Childhood, 1821-1838

Life in Edgefield and Augusta

Though born in Edgefield District, South Carolina, James spent most of his youth in Augusta, Georgia (and later, some time in Somerville, Alabama). It is said that James' father was so impressed by his son's "rocklike" character that he nicknamed him "Peter" (as in "Peter the Rock" of the Bible), leading to him being known as "Pete" or "Old Pete" for much of his life.

Given his son's rocklike character, Longstreet's father charted a course for his son's future. According to Longstreet, "From my early boyhood he conceived that he would send me to West Point for army service." Early on, James' father chose the military life for his son but knew that the local educational system was much too inadequate to provide a good academic background. So in 1830, at the age of nine, James was sent to live with his aunt and uncle in Augusta; his uncle, Augustus Baldwin Longstreet, was a newspaper editor, educator, and Methodist minister. James spent the next eight years on his uncle's plantation, "Westover," while attending the Academy of Richmond County.

In 1833 when James was just twelve, his father died during a cholera epidemic while visiting Augusta. Although James' mother and the remainder of the family then moved to Somerville, Alabama, James remained with Uncle Augustus.

Though his father was gone, young James' resolve for a military life was not. In 1837, Augustus attempted to secure an appointment for James to the United States Military Academy at West Point, New York, but the vacancy for his congressional district had already been filled. A year later James got an appointment through another relative, Reuben Chapman, a Representative from the First District of Alabama (where his mother Mary lived).

Chapter 3: Formal Education, 1830-1842

Academy of Richmond County: 1830-1838

While living and working on his Uncle Augustus' plantation in Augusta, Georgia, James spent eight years attending the Academy of Richmond County (and was no doubt greatly influenced by his uncle, who was himself an educator).

In his memoirs, however, Longstreet barely mentions his academic schooling, heading almost straight into a discussion about his West Point years in the first chapter of the memoirs. Some may take that as an indication he wasn't terribly interested in these early years, but it's just as likely that because he was writing the memoirs to rebut and attack his critics, he wanted to spend as little time as possible discussing pre-military life.

West Point Military Academy: 1838-1842

In 1838, at the age of seventeen, James was appointed to West Point Military Academy in New York, where he proved to be a very poor student academically, as well as a disciplinary problem.

Longstreet explained why he had academic problems: "As cadet I had more interest in the school of the soldier, horsemanship, sword exercise, and the outside game of foot-ball than in the academic courses. The studies were successfully passed, however, until the third year, when I failed in mechanics. When I came to the problem of the pulleys, it seemed to my mind that a soldier could not find use for such appliances, and the pulleys were passed by. At the January examination I was called to the blackboard and given the problem of the pulleys. The drawing from memory of recitation of classmates was good enough, but the demonstration failed to satisfy the sages of the Academic Board. It was the custom, however, to give those who failed in the general examination a second hearing, after all of the classes were examined. This gave me two days to "cram" mechanics, and particularly on pulleys. But the professors were too wily to introduce them a second time, and took me through a searching examination of the six months course. The bridge was safely passed, however, and mechanics left behind. At the June examination, the end of the academic year, I was called to demonstrate the pulleys. The professor thought that I had forgotten my old friend the enemy, but I smiled, for he had become dear to me,--in waking hours and in dreams,--and the cadet passed easily enough for a maximum mark."

James also found other ways to earn scorn: "The cadets had their small joys and sometimes little troubles. On one occasion a cadet officer reported me for disobedience of orders. As the report was not true, I denied it and sent up witnesses of the occasion. Dick Garnett, who fell in the assault of the 3d, at Gettysburg, was one witness, and Cadet Baker, so handsome and lovable that he was called Betsy, was the other. Upon overlooking the records I found the report still there, and went to ask the superintendent if other evidence was necessary to show that the report was not true. He was satisfied of that, but said that the officer complained that I smiled contemptuously. As that could only be rated as a single demerit, I asked the benefit of the smile; but the report stands to this day, Disobedience of orders and three demerits. The cadet had his revenge, however, for the superintendent was afterwards known as The Punster."

Though popular with the other students (befriended by a number of future prominent Civil War figures, including George Henry Thomas, William S. Rosecrans, John Pope, D. H. Hill, Lafayette McLaws, George Pickett, and Ulysses S. Grant), the nearly 6' 2", 200 lb James racked up too many academic and disciplinary problems to receive high ranks. As a result, when he graduated in 1842, he finished third last in his class.

Upon graduation, James was commissioned brevet Second Lieutenant James Longstreet of the Fourth U.S. Infantry and sent to Jefferson Barracks, Missouri.

In his memoirs, Longstreet notes some of the West Point connections that were made by future Civil War generals, aside from his own. It was Longstreet's friendship with Grant that eventually allowed him to play a role in Grant's Republican administration after the war, which was viewed as almost treasonous by some of his former Confederate comrades.

Longstreet also points out that P.G.T. Beauregard and Irvin McDowell, the two commanding officers at the First Battle of Bull Run, went to West Point together. Beauregard's artillery instructor was Robert Anderson, who was in command of the garrison at Fort Sumter when Beauregard ordered the attack on it April 12, 1861, the first fighting of the Civil War.

. In 1846, a shy kid named Thomas Jonathan Jackson made few friends and struggled with his studies, finishing 17th in his class 15 years before becoming Stonewall, while George Pickett was more preoccupied with playing hooky at a local bar before finishing last in the same class as Jackson. The Class of 1846 also included A.P. Hill, who was already in love with the future wife of George McClellan, a young prodigy who finished second in the class of 1846. Years earlier, a clerical error by West Point administrators ensured that Hiram Ulysses Grant forever became known as Ulysses S. Grant. And years after Robert E. Lee met Albert Sidney Johnston and Jefferson Davis at West Point, William Tecumseh Sherman was roommates with George H. Thomas, who later became one of his principal subordinates and the "Rock of Chickamauga".

Chapter 4: Early Life, 1842-1848

Early Military Life

Brevet Second Lieutenant James Longstreet spent his first two years of military service at Jefferson Barracks, Missouri, where he was soon joined by his West Point friend, Lieutenant Ulysses S. Grant. Longstreet pointed out in his memoirs that he loved his assignment, but not for military reasons. "I was fortunate in the assignment to Jefferson Barracks, for in those days the young officers were usually sent off among the Indians or as near the borders as they could find habitable places. In the autumn of 1842 I reported to the company commander, Captain Bradford R. Alden, a most exemplary man, who proved a lasting, valued friend. Eight companies of the Third Infantry were added to the garrison during the spring of 1843, which made garrison life and society gay for the young people and interesting for the older classes. All of the troops were recently from service in the swamps and Everglades of Florida, well prepared to enjoy the change from the war-dance of the braves to the hospitable city of St. Louis; and the graceful step of its charming belles became a joy forever."

Longstreet even recalls being with Grant when he met his wife Julia, writing, "Of the class of 1843, Ulysses S. Grant joined the Fourth Regiment as brevet lieutenant, and I had the pleasure to ride with him on our first visit to Mr. Frederick Dent's home, a few miles from the garrison, where we first met Miss Julia Dent, the charming woman who, five years later, became Mrs. Grant. Miss Dent was a frequent visitor at the garrison balls and hops, where Lieutenant Hoskins, who was something of a tease, would inquire of her if she could tell where he might find "the small lieutenant with the large epaulettes."

Grant

Early Personal Life

Marriage

In 1847, while serving in the Mexican-American War, Major Longstreet met Maria Louisa Garland (called "Louise" by her family), the daughter of Longstreet's regimental commander, Lt. Colonel John Garland.

Married in March of 1848 (one month after the conclusion of the war), the couple had ten children together (only five of whom lived to adulthood): John G. (1848-1918), Augustus Baldwin (1850-1862), William Dent (1853-1854), James (1857-1862), Mary Anne (1860-1862), Robert Lee (1863-1940), James (1865-1922), Fitz Randolph (1869-1951), Louise Longstreet Whelchel (1872-1957), and an unnamed child presumed to have died at birth.

Although their marriage would last over 40 years, Longstreet never mentioned Louise in his memoirs, and most of what is known today about their relationship came from the writings of his second wife, Helen Dortch Longstreet.

Familial Association With U. S. Grant

At about the same time that Longstreet began courting Maria Louisa Garland, Longstreet's West Point friend and fellow Jefferson Barracks comrade Ulysses S. Grant met and began a relationship with Longstreet's fourth cousin, Julia Dent, with the couple marrying on August 22,

1848 in St. Louis, Missouri.

While historians agree that Longstreet attended the Grant-Dent wedding, his specific role during the ceremony remains unclear. Grant biographer Jean Edward Smith asserts that Longstreet served as Grant's Best Man, while John Y. Simon, editor of Julia Grant's memoirs, states that Longstreet "may have been a groomsman."[1] But as Longstreet biographer Donald Brigman Sanger points out, neither Grant nor Longstreet mentioned the role of "Best Man" in either of their memoirs or other personal writings.

Chapter 5: The Mexican-American War, 1846-1848

Contreras, Churubusco, Molino del Rey, Chapultepec

Sent into the action sometime in 1846, Second Lieutenant Longstreet served with distinction in the Mexican-American War with the Eighth U. S. Infantry, receiving brevet promotions to captain for the battles at Contreras and Churubusco, and major for the action at Molino del Rey-- having been cited for gallant and meritorious conduct numerous times.

In the Battle of Chapultepec, September 12-13, 1847, Major Longstreet was severely wounded in the thigh with a musket ball while charging up the hill carrying his regimental colors. Naturally, the color bearer who holds the flag marches front and center and is unarmed, making it the most dangerous position in 19th century warfare, and one that requires incredible bravery. As the incident is recorded, upon falling, Longstreet handed the flag to his friend, a young Lieutenant who finished last in his West Point class of 1846, George E. Pickett. Pickett earned distinction for reaching the summit during the battle, and both men earned reputations at Mexico that would allow them to command brigades early in the Civil War.

Longstreet and General Winfield Scott Hancock (whose performance at Gettysburg during Pickett's Charge on Day 3 was crucial for the Union's success) fought together in the Battle of Churubusco.

There is no question that Longstreet made a name for himself in Mexico, and it was a reputation that would help earn him command over a brigade right at the outset of the Civil War. Yet Longstreet barely mentions his actual service during the Mexican-American war in his memoirs, instead recalling the politics behind the war and two heroic vignettes about other men he fought with in battle. Again, readers can quickly get the sense that he considered Mexico cursory to his life and legacy.

---

[1]   Sanger, Donald B., and Thomas Robson Hay. *James Longstreet, I: Soldier.* Page 13.

Chapter 6: The War Cloud, 1848-1861

After the Mexican-American War and his recovery from the wound sustained at Chapultepec, Longstreet served on routine frontier duty in Texas, primarily at Forts Martin Scott (near Fredericksburg) and Bliss (in El Paso). During this time, Longstreet advanced to the rank of major, mostly performing scouting missions.

Beginning in July of 1858, he began serving as paymaster for the Eighth Infantry. Author Kevin Phillips of *The Cousins' Wars* claims that during this period, Longstreet was involved in a plot to draw the Mexican state of Chihuahua into the Union as a slave state.

As Longstreet put it, "I was stationed at Albuquerque, New Mexico, as paymaster in the United States army when the war-cloud appeared in the East. Officers of the Northern and Southern States were anxious to see the portending storm pass by or disperse, and on many occasions we, too, were assured, by those who claimed to look into the future, that the statesman would yet show himself equal to the occasion, and restore confidence among the people." Clearly Longstreet at the time was hoping for some sort of grand compromise that would avert war.

By the Fall of 1860, however, everyone could see the "war-cloud" on the horizon. With the election of Republican candidate Abraham Lincoln as president on November 6, 1860, many Southerners considered it the final straw. Someone they knew as a "Black Republican" was now set to be inaugurated as President in March.

Throughout the fall and winter of 1860, Southern calls for secession became increasingly serious. In a last-ditched effort to save the Union, Kentucky's Senator John Crittenden tried to assume the stateliness of his predecessor Henry Clay. Crittenden, however, proved to be no Henry Clay: his proposal that a Constitutional Amendment reinstate the Missouri Compromise line and extend it to the Pacific failed. President Buchanan supported the measure, but President-Elect Lincoln said he refused to allow the further expansion of slavery under any conditions.

The Crittenden Compromise failed on December 18. Two days later, South Carolina seceded from the Union. President Buchanan sat on his hands, believing the Southern states had no right to secede, but that the Federal government had no effective power to prevent secession. In January, Mississippi, Florida, Alabama, Georgia, Louisiana and Kansas followed South Carolina's lead. The Confederacy was formed on February 4th, in Montgomery, Alabama, with former Secretary of War Jefferson Davis as its President. On February 23rd, Texas joined the Confederacy.

Jefferson Davis

In his Inauguration Speech, President Lincoln struck a moderate tone. Unlike most Inauguration Addresses, which are typically followed by balls and a "honeymoon" period, Lincoln's came amid a major political crisis. To reassure the South, he reiterated his belief in the legal status of slavery in the South, but that its expansion into the Western territories was to be restricted. He outlined the illegality of secession and refused to acknowledge the South's secession, and promised to continue to deliver U.S. mail in the seceded states. Most importantly, he pledged to not use force unless his obligation to protect Federal property was restricted: "In doing this there needs to be no bloodshed or violence, and there shall be none unless it be forced upon the national authority. The power confided to me will be used to hold, occupy, and posess the property and places belonging to the Government and to collect the duties and imposts; but beyond what may be necessary for these objects, there will be no invasion, no using of force against or among the people anywhere."[2]

Chapter 7: The Civil War Years, 1861 to 1865

Fort Sumter

Lincoln's predecessor was among those who could see the potential conflict coming from a

---

2   "Abraham Lincoln, First Inaugural Address." *Presidents: Every Question Answered.* Page 322.

mile away. As the Confederacy continued to grow during his last months in office, President James Buchanan instructed the federal army to permit the Confederacy to take control of forts in its territory, hoping to avoid a war. Conveniently, this also allowed Southern forces to take control of important forts and land ahead of a potential war, which would make secession and/or a victory in a military conflict easier. Many Southern partisans within the federal government at the end of 1860 took advantage of these opportunities to help Southern states ahead of time.

One of the forts in the South was Fort Sumter, an important but undermanned and undersupplied fort in the harbor of Charleston, South Carolina. Buchanan attempted to resupply Fort Sumter in the first few months of 1860, but the attempt failed when Southern sympathizers in the harbor fired on the resupply ship.

Lincoln had promised that it would not be the North that started a potential war, but he was also aware of the possibility of the South initiating conflict. After he was sworn in, Lincoln sent word to the Governor of South Carolina that he was sending ships to resupply Fort Sumter, to which the governor replied demanding that federal forces evacuate it.

Although he vowed not to fire the first shot, Lincoln was likely aware that his attempt to resupply Fort Sumter in Charleston Harbor would draw Southern fire; it had already happened under Buchanan's watch. After his inauguration, President Lincoln informed South Carolina governor Francis Pickens that he was sending supplies to the undermanned garrison at Fort Sumter. When Lincoln made clear that he would attempt to resupply the fort, Davis ordered Beauregard to demand its surrender and prevent the resupplying of the garrison.

In early April, the ship Lincoln sent to resupply the fort was fired upon and turned around. On April 9, Confederate President Davis sent word to General Beauregard to demand the fort's evacuation. At the time, the federal garrison consisted of Major Robert Anderson, Beauregard's artillery instructor from West Point, and 76 troops. Even before the bombardment, upon learning that he was opposed by Beauregard, Anderson remarked that the Southern forces in Charleston harbor would be exercised with "skill and sound judgment". Beauregard also remembered his former superior, and before the bombardment, he sent brandy, whiskey and cigars to Anderson and his garrison, gifts the Major refused.

At 4:30 a.m. on the morning of April 12, 1861, Beauregard ordered the first shots to be fired at Fort Sumter, effectively igniting the Civil War. After nearly 34 hours and thousands of rounds fired from 47 artillery guns and mortars ringing the harbor, on April 14, 1861, Major Anderson surrendered Fort Sumter, marking the first Confederate victory. No casualties were suffered on either side during the dueling bombardments across Charleston harbor, but, ironically, two Union soldiers were killed by an accidental explosion during the surrender ceremonies.

Beauregard

Although Major James Longstreet was not enthusiastic about the idea of states' secession from the Union, he had learned from his uncle Augustus about the doctrine of states' rights early in his life and seen his uncle's passion for it.

Historically-speaking, there are two quite divergent accounts of Longstreet's entry into the Confederate Army at the start of the War. One states that although born in South Carolina and reared in Georgia, Longstreet offered his services to the state of Alabama (which had appointed him to West Point and where his mother had lived). Thus, as the senior West Point graduate from that state, he was automatically commissioned a rank commensurate with that state's policy. Other accounts, however, assert that Longstreet deliberately traveled to Richmond, Virginia - not Alabama - and offered his services as a paymaster of the new Confederate army. Perhaps, both scenarios are somehow true.

Here's how Longstreet remembered the early days of the Civil War in his memoirs: "When mail-day came the officers usually assembled on the flat roof of the quartermaster's office to look for the dust that in that arid climate announced the coming mail-wagon when five or ten miles away; but affairs continued to grow gloomy, and eventually came information of the attack upon and capture of Fort Sumter by the Confederate forces, which put down speculation and drew the long-dreaded line. A number of officers of the post called to persuade me to remain in the Union service. Captain Gibbs, of the Mounted Rifles, was the principal talker, and after a long but pleasant discussion, I asked him what course he would pursue if his State should pass ordinances of secession and call him to its defence. He confessed that he would obey the call. It was a sad day when we took leave of lifetime comrades and gave up a service of twenty years. Neither Union officers nor their families made efforts to conceal feelings of deepest regret. When we drove out from the post, a number of officers rode with us, which only made the last farewell more trying."

In any regard, on June 17 1861, Major Longstreet resigned from the U. S. Army and on June 22 he met with Confederate President Jefferson Davis at the executive mansion, where he was informed that he had been appointed a brigadier general, a commission he accepted on June 25.

First Bull Run (First Manassas)

After the attack on Fort Sumter, support for both the northern and southern cause rose. Two days later, Lincoln issued a *call-to-arms* asking for 75,000 volunteers. That led to the secession of Virginia, Tennessee, North Carolina, and Arkansas, with the loyalty of border states like Kentucky, Maryland, and Missouri still somewhat up in the air. The large number of southern sympathizers in these states buoyed the Confederates' hopes that those too would soon join the South. Moreover, the loss of these border states, especially Virginia, all deeply depressed Lincoln. Just weeks before, prominent Virginians had reassured Lincoln that the state's historic place in American history made its citizens eager to save the Union. But as soon as Lincoln made any assertive moves to save the Union, Virginia seceded. This greatly concerned Lincoln, who worried Virginia's secession made it more likely other border states and/or Maryland would secede as well.

Despite the loss of Fort Sumter, the North expected a relatively quick victory. Their expectations weren't unrealistic, due to the Union's overwhelming economic advantages over the South. At the start of the war, the Union had a population of over 22 million. The South had a population of 9 million, nearly 4 million of whom were slaves. Union states contained 90% of the manufacturing capacity of the country and 97% of the weapon manufacturing capacity. Union states also possessed over 70% of the total railroads in the pre-war United States at the start of the war, and the Union also controlled 80% of the shipbuilding capacity of the pre-war United States.

However, like William Tecumseh Sherman, Longstreet was among the few who thought the Civil War would last a long time. "Speaking of the impending struggle, I was asked as to the length of the war, and said, 'At least three years, and if it holds for five you may begin to look for a dictator,' at which Lieutenant Ryan, of the Seventh Infantry, said, 'If we are to have a dictator, I hope that you may be the man.'"

Although the North blockaded the South throughout the Civil War and eventually controlled the entire Mississippi River by 1863, the war could not be won without land battles, which doomed hundreds of thousands of soldiers on each side. This is because the Civil War generals began the war employing tactics from the Napoleonic Era, which saw Napoleon dominate the European continent and win crushing victories against large armies. However, the weapons available in 1861 were far more accurate than they had been 50 years earlier. In particular, new rifled barrels created common infantry weapons with deadly accuracy of up to 100 yards, at a time when generals were still leading massed infantry charges with fixed bayonets and attempting to march their men close enough to engage in hand-to-hand combat.

Ordered to report to Brig. General P.G.T. Beauregard at Manassas, Brig. General Longstreet was given command of a brigade of three regiments—the First, Eleventh, and Seventeenth Virginia Infantry. Immediately assembling his staff, Longstreet trained his brigade incessantly and within just a few weeks had trained his "green" recruits in close-order drill and battlefield maneuvers. Though considered a dogged combat trainer and able defensive commander, ultimately, his field tactics would make him the object of great controversy before the War's end.

After Fort Sumter, the Lincoln Administration pushed for a quick invasion of Virginia, with the intent of defeating Confederate forces and marching toward the Confederate capitol of Richmond. Lincoln pressed Irvin McDowell to push forward. Despite the fact that McDowell knew his troops were inexperienced and unready, pressure from the Washington politicians forced him to launch a premature offensive against Confederate forces in Northern Virginia. His strategy during the First Battle of Bull Run was grand, but it proved far too difficult for his inexperienced troops to carry out effectively.

McDowell

In late Spring 1861, Davis ordered Beauregard to northern Virginia as second-in-command to General Joseph E. Johnston, where he was to oppose the federal forces building up under

McDowell. Though Johnston was the superior in rank, he ceded authority to Beauregard near Manassas Junction, leaving Beauregard in command there. At Manassas, Beauregard took charge of the Confederate forces assembling near the rail junction at Manassas and had his men construct defenses along a 14 mile front along Bull Run Creek. Meanwhile, Johnston was gathering and training additional troops in the Shenandoah Valley.

Joseph E. Johnston

McDowell's strategy during the First Battle of Bull Run was grand, and in many ways it was the forerunner of a tactic Lee and Jackson executed brilliantly on nearly the same field during the Second Battle of Bull Run or Manassas in August 1862. McDowell's plan called for parts of his army to pin down Beauregard's Confederate soldiers in front while marching another wing of his army around the flank and into the enemy's rear, rolling up the line. McDowell assumed the Confederates would be forced to abandon Manassas Junction and fall back to the next defensible line, the Rappahannock River. In July 1861, however, this proved far too difficult for his inexperienced troops to carry out effectively.

On July 18, Union General Irwin McDowell set out with two divisions on a twelve-mile circuitous march west from Centreville, Virginia to cross Bull Run at Sudley Springs Ford, intending to strike Beauregard's troops at Manassas-Sudley Road in an effort to turn the Southern left flank. Meanwhile, another division was set to drive directly west along the turnpike and across Stone Bridge, while back at Centreville, another division stayed in reserve. The remaining division, scattered along the lines of communication all the way back to

Washington but would ultimately take no part in the ensuing battle, made a total of 32,000 men at McDowell's disposal.

Longstreet's new recruits achieved one of the first Confederate victories, seeing action at Blackburn's Ford on July 18 and successfully stopping the lead Union division in its march towards Manassas. And unbeknownst to McDowell, several days earlier, General Beauregard had received advance warning of troop movement from a civilian and had forwarded a coded message to Jefferson Davis along with a request to move General Joseph E. Johnston and his 12,000 men from the Shenandoah Valley to Manassas, via rail. Beauregard's intelligence placed the Union Army within attack position by July 17.

The First Battle of Bull Run made history in several ways. McDowell's army met Fort Sumter hero P.G.T. Beauregard's Confederate army near the railroad junction at Manassas on July 21, 1861. Located just 25 miles away from Washington D.C., many civilians from Washington came to watch what they expected to be a rout of Confederate forces. And for awhile, it appeared as though that might be the case.

McDowell's strategy fell apart though, thanks to railroads. Confederate reinforcements under General Joseph E. Johnston's Army, including JEB Stuart's cavalrymen and a brigade led by Thomas Jonathan Jackson, arrived by train in the middle of the day, a first in the history of American warfare. With Johnston's army arriving midday on July 21, it evened up the numbers between Union and Confederate. Shoring up the Confederates' left flank, some of Johnston's troops, led by Jackson's brigade, helped reverse the Union's momentum and ultimately turn the tide. As the battle's momentum switched, the inexperienced Union troops were routed and retreated in disorder back toward Washington in an unorganized mass. With over 350 killed on each side, it was the deadliest battle in American history to date, and both the Confederacy and the Union were quickly served notice that the war would be much more costly than either side had believed.

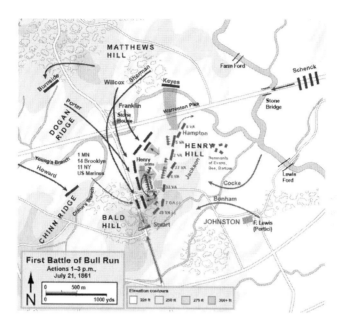

First Battle of Bull Run
Actions 1–3 p.m.,
July 21, 1861

Ironically, McDowell commanded the Army of Northeastern Virginia and Joseph E. Johnston commanded the Army of the Potomac at First Bull Run. A little over a year later it would be Lee's Army of Northern Virginia fighting elements of the Union Army of the Potomac at Second Bull Run, on nearly the same ground.

It was also during First Manassas or Bull Run that Jackson earned the famous nickname "Stonewall", but there is an enduring mystery over the origin of his nickname. What is known is that during the battle, Jackson's brigade arrived as reinforcements at a crucial part of the battlefield on the Confederate left. Confederate Brigadier General Barnard Bee, commanding a nearby brigade, commanded his men to reestablish their battle line next to Jackson's brigade, shouting, "There is Jackson standing like a stone wall. Rally behind the Virginians." General Bee was mortally wounded shortly after that command and died the following day. Thus, it remains unclear whether Bee was complimenting Jackson's brigade for standing firm or whether he was criticizing Jackson's brigade for inaction. Without Bee around to explain his command, nobody will ever know for certain. However, that has not stopped people from debating Bee's comment. Regardless, the nickname Stonewall stuck, and Jackson was henceforth known as Stonewall Jackson. His brigade also inherited the title, known throughout the war as the Stonewall brigade.

Stonewall Jackson

Longstreet's brigade played almost no role in the fighting on July 21, other than having to sustain artillery fire for several hours. But when the Union army was routed and began fleeing in a disorganized panic, Longstreet was incensed that his commanders did not attempt to pursue the disorganized federal troops running back toward Washington. Longstreet's staff officer, Moxley Sorrel, later wrote that Longstreet "dashed his hat furiously to the ground, stamped, and bitter words escaped him."

Nevertheless, a few months later, on October 7, Longstreet was promoted to major general and assumed command of a division in the newly reorganized Confederate Army of Northern Virginia. He was now in command of 4 infantry brigades and Hampton's Legion.

Though he had attained personal success thus far, he suffered personal tragedy in January 1862 due to a scarlet fever epidemic in Richmond that killed his one-year-old daughter Mary Anne, his four-year-old son James, and six-year-old son Augustus ("Gus"), all in the span of a week. Understandably depressed, Longstreet became personally withdrawn and melancholy, turning to religion. Those close to him and who served under him noted the change in camp around him after January 1862. What had once been a boisterous headquarters that tolerated partying and poker games had become a solemn, somber and more devout one.

The Peninsula Campaign, 1862

Despite Union successes in the Western theater, the focus of the Lincoln Administration remained concentrated on Richmond. The loss at Bull Run prompted a changing of the guard, with George McClellan, the "Young Napoleon", put in charge of reorganizing and leading the

Army of the Potomac. McClellan had finished second in his class at West Point and was a well-regarded engineer, not to mention a foreign observer at the siege of Sevastopol during the Crimean War. This experience made him fit for commanding an army, but it also colored his military ideology in a way that was at odds with a Lincoln Administration that was eager for aggressive action and movement toward Richmond.

Under McClellan, and at Lincoln's urging, the Army of the Potomac conducted an ambitious amphibious invasion of Virginia in the spring of 1862. McClellan hoped to circumvent Confederate defenses to the north of Richmond by attacking Richmond from the southeast, landing his giant army on the Virginian peninsula. McClellan originally surprised the Confederates with his movement, but the narrow peninsula made it easier for Confederate forces to defend. One heavily outnumbered force led by John Magruder famously held out under siege at Yorktown for nearly an entire month, slowing the Army of the Potomac down. Magruder used a tactic of marching his men up and down the siege lines repeatedly to give the appearance he had several times more men than he actually had.

General Magruder

Commanding Confederate forces opposing McClellan was General Joseph E. Johnston. During the Civil War, one of the tales that was often told among Confederate soldiers was that Joseph E. Johnston was a crack shot who was a better bird hunter than just about everyone else in the South. However, as the story went, Johnston would never take the shot when asked to, complaining that something was wrong with the situation that prevented him from being able to shoot the bird when it was time. The story is almost certainly apocryphal, used to demonstrate the Confederates' frustration with a man who everyone regarded as a capable general. Johnston began the Civil War as one of the senior commanders, leading (ironically) the Army of the Potomac to victory in the Battle of First Bull Run over Irvin McDowell's Union Army. But Johnston would become known more for losing by not winning. Johnston was never badly beaten in battle, but he had a habit of "strategically withdrawing" until he had nowhere else to go.

Johnston gradually pulled his troops back to a line of defense nearer Richmond as McClellan advanced. Several weeks later, after word of General Stonewall Jackson's startling victories in the Shenandoah Valley were received, Johnston learned that McClellan was moving along the Chickahominy River. McClellan's Army of the Potomac got close enough to Richmond that they could see the city's church steeples.

It was at this point that Johnston got uncharacteristically aggressive. Johnston had run out of breathing space for his army, and he believed McCellan was seeking to link up with McDowell's forces. Therefore he drew up a very complex plan of attack for different wings of his army, and struck at the Army of the Potomac at the Battle of Seven Pines on May 31, 1862. Like McDowell's plan for First Bull Run, the plan proved too complicated for Johnston's army to execute, and after a day of bloody fighting little was accomplished from a technical standpoint. However, McClellan was rattled by the attack, and Johnston was seriously wounded during the fighting, resulting in military advisor Robert E. Lee being sent to assume command of the Army of Northern Virginia.

Lee

From his first day in command, Lee faced a daunting, seemingly impossible challenge.

McClellan had maneuvered nearly 100,000 troops to within seven miles of Richmond, three Union units were closing in on General Jackson's Confederates in Virginia's Shenandoah Valley, and a fourth Union army was camped on the Rappahannock River ostensibly ready to come to McClellan's aid.

In a series of confrontations known as the Seven Days' Battle, Lee instructed Jackson to move as if to advance back through the Shenandoah Valley but then secretly bring his entire force by train back to the Richmond sector as reinforcements. Jackson had successfully tied up the Union armies in the Valley before returning to Richmond. Lee immediately took the offensive, attacking the Army of the Potomac repeatedly in a flurry of battles known as the Seven Days Battles. Fearing he was heavily outnumbered, McClellan began a strategic retreat, and despite badly defeating the Confederates at the Battle of Malvern Hill, the last battle of the Seven Days Battles and the Peninsula Campaign, it was clear that the Army of the Potomac was quitting the campaign. The failure of McClellan's campaign devastated the morale of the North, as McClellan had failed to advance despite originally having almost double the manpower.

In a characteristically audacious manner that came to define his generalship, Lee's bold offensive tactics had seen his army engage in bloody hand-to-hand combat that ranged from Mechanicsville to Fraser's Farm to Malvern Hill. By themselves, none of the battles could be called pivotal or even tactical victories for the Confederates, and Malvern Hill was a debacle, but from a strategic standpoint Lee succeeded in forcing McClellan and his back-up forces to retreat, while Jackson's tactics proved effective in the Shenandoah. Lee had prevented McClellan from capturing Richmond.

Longstreet had done well as a rear guard commander at Yorktown and Williamsburg, successfully delaying the advance of Union Maj. General George B. McClellan's army toward Richmond, but during the Battle of Seven Pines, he marched his men in the wrong direction down the wrong road, causing congestion and confusion among other Confederate units and ultimately weakening the effectiveness of the massive Confederate counterattack launched against McClellan. In his official report, Longstreet blamed fellow Maj. General Benjamin Huger for the logistical confusion, an indication of the contention that would follow his personal and military life from that time on.

During the Seven Days Battles, Longstreet was more effective. In command of an entire wing of Lee's army, Longstreet aggressively attacked at Gaines' Mill and Glendale. Historians have credited Longstreet for those battles and criticized Stonewall Jackson for being unusually lethargic during the Seven Days Battles, ultimately contributing to Lee's inability to do more damage or capture McClellan's Army of the Potomac. Jackson's performance was not lost on Longstreet, who pointed out that he performed poorly at the Seven Days Battles to defend charges that he was slow at Gettysburg.

By the end of the campaign, Longstreet was one of the most popular and praised men in the army. Like Longstreet's father, Sorrel considered him a "rock in steadiness when sometimes in battle the world seemed flying to pieces." General Lee himself called Old Pete "the staff in my right hand." Though it is often forgotten, Longstreet was now Lee's principle subordinate, not Stonewall Jackson.

Longstreet in 1862

Second Bull Run (Second Manassas)

Even before McClellan had completely withdrawn his troops, Lee sent Jackson northward to intercept the new army Abraham Lincoln had placed under Maj. General John Pope, formed out of the scattered troops in the Virginia area. Pope had found success in the Western theater, and he was uncommonly brash, instructing the previously defeated men now under his command that his soldiers in the West were accustomed to seeing the backs of the enemy. Pope's arrogance turned off his own men, and it also caught the notice of Lee.

Once certain McClellan was in full retreat, Lee joined Jackson, planning to strike Pope before McClellan's troops could arrive as reinforcements. In late August 1862, in a "daring and unorthodox" move, Lee divided his forces and sent Jackson northward to flank them, ultimately bringing Jackson directly behind Pope's army and supply base. This forced Pope to fall back to Manassas to protect his flank and maintain his lines of communication. Recognizing Lee's genius for military strategy, General Jackson quickly became Lee's most trusted commander, and he would later say that he so trusted Lee's military instincts that he would even follow him into battle blindfolded.

When Pope's army fell back to Manassas to confront Jackson, his wing of Lee's army dug in along a railroad trench and took a defensive stance. The Second Battle of Manassas or Bull Run was fought August 28-30, beginning with the Union army throwing itself at Jackson the first two days. But the concentration on Stonewall's men opened up the Union army's left flank for Longstreet's wing, which marched 30 miles in 24 hours to reach the battlefield by the late afternoon of August 29. When Longstreet's men finally arrived around noon on August 29, Lee informed Longstreet of his plan to attack the Union flank--which was at that time concentrating its efforts on General Jackson. Longstreet initially rejected Lee's suggestion to attack, recommending instead that a reconnaissance be conducted to survey the field. And although Longstreet's artillery was ultimately a major factor in helping Jackson resist the Union attack on August 29, his performance that day was described by some Lost Cause advocates as slow, and they considered his disobedience of General Lee insubordination. Lee's most famous biographer, Douglas Southall Freeman, later wrote: "The seeds of much of the disaster on July 2, 1863, at the Battle of Gettysburg were sown in that instant—when Lee yielded to Longstreet and Longstreet discovered that he would."[3]

Nevertheless, the Second Battle of Bull Run or Manassas is considered one of Longstreet's most successful. While Jackson's men defended themselves the first two days, Lee used Longstreet's wing on August 30 to deliver a devastating flank attack before reinforcements from the retreating Army of the Potomac could reach the field. With over 25,000 men, Longstreet's attack lasted several hours, while he and Lee were in the thick of things directing brigades and artillery batteries while coming under fire themselves. Eventually, Longstreet's attack swept Pope's army off the field. Fought on the same ground as the First Battle of Manassas nearly a year earlier, the result was the same: a decisive Confederate victory that sent Union soldiers scrambling back to the safety of Washington. Longstreet called Lee's campaign "clever and brilliant", and it helped reinforce the belief that using offensive marching and defensive battle tactics (like having Jackson's wing flank Pope's army and forcing Pope to attack it) was the key to success.

---

[3]   Tagg, Larry. *The Generals of Gettysburg*. Page 205.

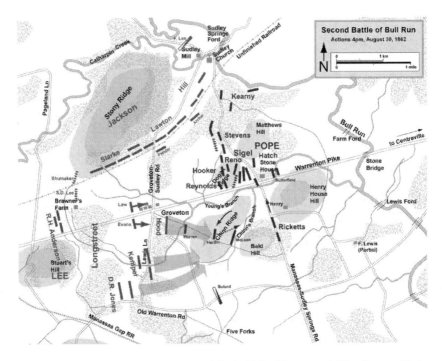

After the battle, General Lafayette McLaws (who had joined Longstreet's First Corps as First Division Commander and subsequently stayed with Longstreet for most of the War) assessed Longstreet unapologetically, saying, "James Longstreet is a humbug--a man of small capacity who is very obstinate, not at all chivalrous, exceedingly conceited, and entirely selfish!"[4] Thus it seems that Longstreet's propensity for friction was apparent long before that fateful day at Gettysburg.

Antietam (Sharpsburg)

After two days' fighting, Lee had achieved another major victory, and he now stood unopposed 12 miles away from Washington D.C. While Johnston and Beauregard had stayed in this position in the months after the first battle, Lee determined upon a more aggressive course: taking the fighting to the North.

In early September, convinced that the best way to defend Richmond was to divert attention to

---

4   Garrison, Webb. *Civil War Curiosities*. Page 236.

Washington, Lee had decided to invade Maryland after obtaining Jefferson Davis's permission. Today the decision is remembered through the prism of Lee hoping to win a major battle in the North that would bring about European recognition of the Confederacy, potential intervention, and possible capitulation by the North, whose anti-war Democrats were picking up political momentum. However, Lee also hoped that the fighting in Maryland would relieve Virginia's resources, especially the Shenandoah Valley, which served as the state's "breadbasket". And though largely forgotten today, Lee's move was controversial among his own men. Confederate soldiers, including Lee, took up arms to defend their homes, but now they were being asked to invade a Northern state. An untold number of Confederate soldiers refused to cross the Potomac River into Maryland.

Despite that, Longstreet also held the same view as Lee, believing an invasion of Maryland had plenty of advantages. He wrote in his memoirs, "The Army of Northern Virginia was afield without a foe. Its once grand adversary, discomfited under two commanders, had crept into cover of the bulwarks about the national capital. The commercial, social, and blood ties of Maryland inclined her people to the Southern cause. A little way north of the Potomac were inviting fields of food and supplies more plentiful than on the southern side; and the fields for march and manoeuvre, strategy and tactics, were even more inviting than the broad fields of grain and comfortable pasture-lands. Propitious also was the prospect of swelling our ranks by Maryland recruits."

In the summer of 1862, the Union suffered more than 20,000 casualties, and Northern Democrats, who had been split into pro-war and anti-war factions from the beginning, increasingly began to question the war. As of September 1862, no progress had been made on Richmond; in fact, a Confederate army was now in Maryland. And with the election of 1862 was approaching, Lincoln feared the Republicans might suffer losses in the congressional midterms that would harm the war effort. Thus, he restored General McClellan and removed General Pope after the second disaster at Bull Run. McClellan was still immensely popular among the Army of the Potomac, and with a mixture of men from his Army of the Potomac and Pope's Army of Virginia, he began a cautious pursuit of Lee into Maryland.

McClellan

Historians believe that Lee's entire Army of Northern Virginia had perhaps 50,000 men at most and possibly closer to 30,000 during the Maryland campaign. However, Lee sized up George McClellan, figured he was a cautious general, and decided once again to divide his forces throughout Maryland. In early September, he ordered Jackson to capture Harpers Ferry while he and Longstreet maneuvered his troops toward Frederick. With McClellan now assuming command of the Northern forces, Lee expected to have plenty of time to assemble his troops and bring his battle plan to fruition.

However, the North was about to have one of the greatest strokes of luck during the Civil War. For reasons that are still unclear, Union troops in camp at Frederick came across a copy of Special Order 191, wrapped up among three cigars. The order contained Lee's entire marching plans for Maryland, making it clear that the Army of Northern Virginia had been divided into multiple parts, which, if faced by overpowering strength, could be entirely defeated and bagged. The "Lost Order" quickly made its way to General McClellan, who took several hours to debate whether or not it was intentional misinformation or actually real. Once he decided it was accurate, McClellan is said to have famously boasted, "Here is a paper with which if I cannot whip Bobby Lee, I will be willing to go home."

To Lee's great surprise, McClellan's army began moving at an uncharacteristically quick pace, pushing in on his Confederate forces at several mountain passes at South Mountain, including at Turner's Gap and Crampton's Gap. While Jackson's wing was forcing the Harpers Ferry garrison to surrender, Lee regathered his other scattered units around Sharpsburg near Antietam Creek. McClellan's army, which may have outnumbered Lee's forces by about 50,000 men, confronted the Confederates around the night of September 16.

Longstreet described the scene before the battle commenced: "The blue uniforms of the federals appeared among the trees that crowned the heights on the eastern bank of the Antietam. The number increased, and larger and larger grew the field of blue until is seemed to stretch as far as the eye could see, and from the tops of the mountains down to the edge of the stream gathered the great army of McClellan."[5]

As fate would have it, the bloodiest day in the history of the United States took place on the 75th anniversary of the signing of the Constitution. On September 17, 1862, Lee's Army of Northern Virginia fought McClellan's Army of the Potomac outside Sharpsburg along Antietam Creek. That day, nearly 25,000 would become casualties, and Lee's army barely survived fighting the much bigger Northern army. The fighting that morning started with savage fighting on the Confederate left flank near Dunker church, in a corn field and forests. The Confederates barely held the field in the north sector.

Lee's army may have been saved by the Northern army's inability to cross the creek near "Burnside's Bridge". Ambrose Burnside had been given command of the "Right Wing" of the Army of the Potomac (the I Corps and IX Corps) at the start of the Maryland Campaign for the Battle of South Mountain, but McClellan separated the two corps at the Battle of Antietam, placing them on opposite ends of the Union battle line. However, Burnside continued to act as though he was a wing commander instead of a corps commander, so instead of ordering the IX corps, he funneled orders through General Jacob D. Cox. This poor organization contributed to the corps's hours-long delay in attacking and crossing what is now called "Burnside's Bridge" on the right flank of the Confederate line.

General Burnside

[5]   Gaffney, P., and D. Gaffney. *The Civil War: Exploring History One Week at a Time.* Page 179.

Making matters worse, Burnside did not perform adequate reconnaissance of the area, which afforded several easy fording sites of the creek out of range of the Army of Northern Virginia. Instead of unopposed crossings, his troops were forced into repeated assaults across the narrow bridge which was dominated by Confederate sharpshooters on high ground across the bridge. The delay allowed General A.P. Hill's Confederate division to reach the battlefield from Harpers Ferry in time to save Lee's right flank that afternoon. Fearing that his army was badly bloodied and figuring Lee had many more men than he did, McClellan refused to commit his reserves to continue the attacks. The day ended in a tactical stalemate.

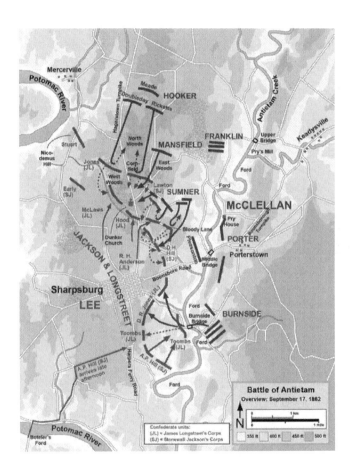

Though badly beaten and out of supplies, Lee somehow managed to withdraw his troops across the Potomac and back to safety. Though his invasion of Maryland had been a total failure, to his credit, it was only by his military prowess that he was able to save his army and maintain the integrity of the Confederate forces. Nevertheless, Antietam is now widely considered a turning point in the war. Although the battle was tactically a draw, it resulted in forcing Lee's army out of Maryland and back into Virginia, making it a strategic victory for the North and an opportune time for President Abraham Lincoln to issue the Emancipation Proclamation.

Dead soldiers along the turnpike at Antietam. Antietam was the first battle in which war dead were photographed and made publicly available, stunning Americans.

Although Lee and Jackson would ultimately receive the lion's share of credit for stopping McClellan's advance, it had been Longstreet's men who had held Lee's position long enough on the left and middle for Jackson to arrive and administer damage. One account describes Longstreet as coming upon an abandoned piece of artillery during one of the assaults, jumping off his horse, and then manning the gun himself for a half hour as his men kept reloading.

The same day as the Battle of Antietam, the *Washington Star* erroneously reported, "At the latest advices everything was favorable. Gen. Longstreet was reported killed and [General] Daniel Harvey Hill taken prisoner."[6] Later that same day, the *Star* dispatched, "Gen. Longstreet was wounded and is a prisoner." All of that was incorrect.

Fredericksburg (Marye's Heights)

Despite heavily outnumbering the Southern army and badly damaging it during the battle of Antietam, McClellan decided not to pursue Lee across the Potomac, citing shortages of equipment and the fear of overextending his forces. General-in-Chief Henry W. Halleck wrote in his official report, "The long inactivity of so large an army in the face of a defeated foe, and during the most favorable season for rapid movements and a vigorous campaign, was a matter of great disappointment and regret." Lincoln had also had enough of McClellan's constant excuses for not taking forward action, and he relieved McClellan of his command of the Army of the Potomac on November 7, effectively ending the general's military career.

In place of McClellan, Lincoln appointed Burnside, who had just failed at Antietam. Burnside didn't believe he was competent to command the entire army, a very honest (and accurate) judgment. However, Burnside also didn't want the command to fall upon Joe Hooker, who had been injured while aggressively fighting with his I Corps at Antietam in the morning. Thus, he accepted.

Under pressure from Lincoln to be aggressive, Burnside laid out a difficult plan to cross the Rappahannock and attack the Confederates near Fredericksburg. The plan was doomed from the very beginning. On December 12, Burnside's army struggled to cross the river under fire from Confederate sharpshooters in the town. The next day, the Army of the Potomac could not dislodge Stonewall Jackson's men on the right flank.

The battle is mostly remembered however for the piecemeal attacks the Union army made on heavily fortified positions Longstreet's men took up on Marye's Heights. With the massacre at Antietam still fresh in his mind (partially caused by the Confederates having not constructed defensive works), Longstreet ordered trenches, abatis (obstacles formed by felled trees with sharpened branches), and fieldworks to be constructed - which to Longstreet's credit, set a precedent for all future defensive battles of the Army of Northern Virginia. To his thinking, if the artillery didn't keep Union forces at bay, the twenty-five hundred Confederates lined up four-deep behind a quarter-mile long four-foot stone wall would deter even the most foolhardy. Thus when it was learned that General Burnside was planning a direct assault on "the Heights," even

---

[6]   Stepp, John, W. and Hill, William I. (editors). *Mirror of War, The Washington Star Reports the Civil War.* Page 151.

the other Union generals couldn't believe it.

As they threw themselves at Longstreet's heavily fortified position along the high ground, the Northern soldiers were mowed down again and again. General Longstreet compared the near continuous fall of soldiers on the battlefield to "the stead dripping of rain from the eaves of a house."[7] Still, Burnside sent wave after wave up the hill, with the Union injured (or those just cowering in the field) trying to stop the advancing men by grabbing at their legs and feet-- begging them to turn back. In the end, a recorded 14 assaults were made on Marye's Heights, all of which failed, with over 12,650 Union soldiers killed, wounded, or gone missing. Despite all their efforts, not one Union soldier got within 100 feet of the wall at Marye's Heights before being shot or forced to withdraw. And although General Longstreet is credited with assuring a Confederate victory, many historians characterize the battle as "murder, not warfare."

As men lay dying on the field that night, the Northern Lights made a rare appearance. Southern soldiers took it as a divine omen and wrote about it frequently in their diaries. The Union soldiers saw less divine inspiration in the Northern Lights and mentioned it less in their own. The Battle of Fredericksburg also spawned one of Lee's most memorable quotes. During the battle, Lee turned to Longstreet and commented, "It is well that war is so terrible, otherwise we would grow too fond of it."[8]

---

[7]   Gaffney, P. and D. Gaffney. *The Civil War: Exploring History One Week at a Time.* Page 201

[8]   Nagel, Paul C. *The Lee's of Virginia.* Page 179.

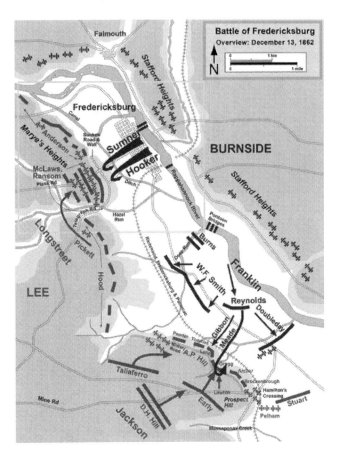

After the virtual slaughter (with the dead said to have been stacked up in rows), the Union army retreated across the river in defeat. Although Lee had accomplished a decisive victory over Burnside's forces, the Union general had positioned his reserves and supply line so strategically that he could easily fall back without breaking lines of communication--while Lee had no such reserves or supplies. And since Lee didn't have the men to pursue and completely wipe out Burnside's army (and simply holding them would ultimately prove too costly), Lee chose not to give chase. Some military strategists contend this was a military blunder, but either way, the fighting in 1862 was done.

Chancellorsville

After the Confederate victory at Fredericksburg, Lee dispatched Longstreet and his corps back to the Virginia Peninsula to protect Richmond and gather food and other much-needed supplies. Although Longstreet accomplished both missions, he was later criticized for having not taken advantage of the opportunity to attack Union positions in the area. As had now become Longstreet's *modus operandi*, to deflect responsibility, he simply responded that he didn't think they could afford the "powder and ball"--an assertion many historians fully doubt.

In May of 1863, General Lee ordered Longstreet to rejoin his Army of Northern Virginia in time for a potential battle, which would come at the very beginning of May. Longstreet's men would not reach Chancellorsville in time, but it still ended up being a stunning victory for the Confederates.

Lee had concluded an incredibly successful year for the Confederates in the East, but the South was still struggling. The Confederate forces in the West had failed to win a major battle, suffering defeat at places like Shiloh in Tennessee and across the Mississippi River. As the war continued into 1863, the southern economy continued to deteriorate. Southern armies were suffering serious deficiencies of nearly all supplies as the Union blockade continued to be effective as stopping most international commerce with the Confederacy. Moreover, the prospect of Great Britain or France recognizing the Confederacy had been all but eliminated by the Emancipation Proclamation.

Given the unlikelihood of forcing the North's capitulation, the Confederacy's main hope for victory was to win some decisive victory or hope that Abraham Lincoln would lose his reelection bid in 1864, and that the new president would want to negotiate peace with the Confederacy. Understandably, this colored Confederate war strategy, and unquestionably Lee's.

After the Fredericksburg debacle and the "Mud March" fiasco that left a Union advance literally dead in its tracks, Lincoln fired Burnside and replaced him with "Fighting Joe" Hooker. Hooker had gotten his nickname from a clerical error in a newspaper's description of fighting, but the nickname stuck, and Lee would later playfully refer to him as F.J. Hooker. Hooker had stood out for his zealous fighting at Antietam, and the battle may very well have turned out differently if he hadn't been injured at the head of the I Corps. Now he was in command of a 100,000 man Army of the Potomac, and he devised a complex plan to cross the Rappahannock River with part of his force near Fredericksburg to pin down Lee while using the other bulk to turn Lee's left, which would allow his forces to reach the Confederate rear.

Hooker's plan initially worked perfectly, with the division of his army surprising Lee. Lee was outnumbered two to one and now had to worry about threats on two fronts. Incredibly, Lee once again decided to divide his forces in the face of the enemy, sending Stonewall Jackson to turn the

Union army's right flank while the rest of the army maintained positions near Fredericksburg. The Battle of Chancellorsville is one of the most famous of the Civil War, and the most famous part of the battle was Stonewall Jackson's daring march across the Army of the Potomac's flank, surprising the XI Corps with an attack on May 2, 1863. Having ignored warnings of Jackson's march, the XI Corps was quickly routed.

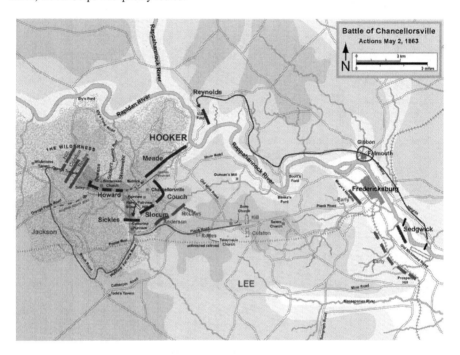

The surprise was a costly success however. Jackson scouted out ahead of his lines later that night and was mistakenly fired upon by his own men, badly wounding him. Jackson's natural replacement, A.P. Hill, was also injured, so Lee had cavalry leader J.E.B. Stuart assume command of Jackson's corps with Jackson out of action. On May 3, Stuart fiercely attacked the Union army, attempting to push them into the river, while on the other flank, the Confederates evacuated from Fredericksburg but ultimately held the line. Hooker began to lose his nerve, and he was injured during the battle when a cannonball nearly killed him. Historians now believe that Hooker may have commanded part of the battle while suffering from a concussion.

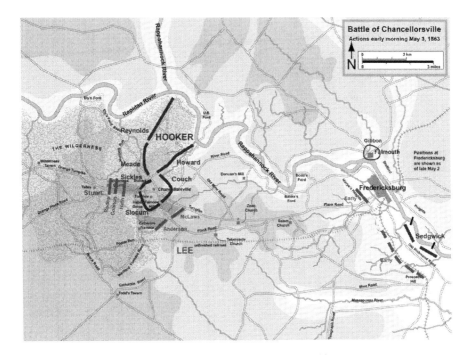

By the end of the battle, the Army of the Potomac had once again been defeated, retreating across the river. But Lee would also lose his "right hand". After Jackson's left arm was amputated, he seemed to be recovering, but his doctors were unaware of his symptoms that indicated oncoming pneumonia. Jackson would die May 10, eight days after his brilliant attack.

Gettysburg

After Chancellorsville, Longstreet and Lee met to discuss options for the Confederate Army's summer campaign. Longstreet advocated detachment of all or part of his corps to be sent to Tennessee, citing Union Maj. General Ulysses S. Grant's advance on Vicksburg, the critical Confederate stronghold on the Mississippi River. Longstreet argued that a reinforced army under Bragg could defeat Rosecrans and drive toward the Ohio River, compelling Grant to release his hold on Vicksburg. Lee, however, was opposed to a division of his army and instead advocated a large-scale offensive (and raid) into Pennsylvania. In addition, General Lee hoped to supply his army on the unscathed fields and towns of the North, while giving war ravaged northern Virginia a rest.

Knowing that victories on Virginia soil meant little to an enemy that could simply retreat, regroup, and then return with more men and more advanced equipment, Lee set his sights on a Northern invasion, aiming to turn Northern opinion against the war and against President Lincoln. Given the right circumstances, Lee's army might even be able to capture either Baltimore or Philadelphia and use the city as leverage in peace negotiations.

In the wake of Jackson's death, Lee reorganized his army, creating three Corps out of the previous two, with A.P. Hill and Richard S. Ewell "replacing" Stonewall. Hill had been a successful division commander, but he was constantly battling bouts of sickness that left him disabled, which would occur at Gettysburg. Ewell had distinguished himself during the Peninsula Campaign, suffering a serious injury that historians often credit as making him more cautious in command upon his return.

With J.E.B. Stuart's cavalry screening his movements, Lee marched his army into Pennsylvania, once again dividing his forces to take different objectives. This time, however, they mostly stayed within a day's marching distance of each other. Meanwhile, the loss at Chancellorsville led to Lincoln relieving Hooker as he was leading the Army of the Potomac in pursuit of Lee. George Meade assumed command of the Army of the Potomac just a few days before the Battle of Gettysburg. Stuart established a reputation as an audacious cavalry commander and on two occasions (during the Peninsula Campaign and the Maryland Campaign) rode around the Army of the Potomac in its rear, bringing fame to himself and embarrassment to the Union generals, especially General McClellan. At the Battle of Chancellorsville, he distinguished himself as a temporary commander of the wounded Stonewall Jackson's infantry corps.

However, Stuart's role at Gettysburg was far more controversial. Given great discretion in his cavalry operations before the battle, Stuart's cavalry was too far removed from the Army of Northern Virginia to warn Lee of the Army of the Potomac's movements. As it would turn out, Lee's army inadvertently stumbled into Union cavalry and then the Union army at Gettysburg on the morning of July 1, 1863, walking blindly into what became the largest battle of the war. Stuart has been heavily criticized ever since, and it is said Lee took him to task when he arrived on the second day, leading Stuart to offer his resignation. Lee didn't accept it, but he would later note in his after battle report that the cavalry had not updated him as to the Army of the Potomac's movements.

It is believed that one of the first notices Lee got about the Army of the Potomac's movements came from a spy named "Harrison", a man who apparently worked undercover for Longstreet but of whom little is known. Harrison reported that General George G. Meade was now in command of the Union Army and was at that very moment marching north to meet Lee's army.

According to Longstreet, he and Lee were supposedly on the same page at the beginning of the campaign. "His plan or wishes announced, it became useless and improper to offer suggestions leading to a different course. All that I could ask was that the policy of the campaign should be one of defensive tactics; that we should work so as to force the enemy to attack us, in such good position as we might find in our own country, so well adapted to that purpose—which might assure us of a grand triumph. To this he readily assented as an important and material adjunct to his general plan." Lee later claimed he "had never made any such promise, and had never thought of doing any such thing," but in his official report after the battle, Lee also noted, "It had not been intended to fight a general battle at such a distance from our base, unless attacked by the enemy.

Day 1

Without question, the most famous battle of the Civil War took place outside of the small town of Gettysburg, Pennsylvania, which happened to be a transporation hub, serving as the center of a wheel with several roads leading out to other Pennsylvanian towns. Lee was unaware of Meade's position when an advanced division of Hill's Corps marched toward Gettysburg on the morning of July 1. The battle began with John Buford's Union cavalry forces skirmishing against the advancing division of Heth's just outside of town. Buford's actions allowed the I Corps of the Army of the Potomac to reach Gettysburg and engage the Confederates, eventually setting the stage for the biggest and most well known battle of the war.

Day 1 by itself would have been one of the 20 biggest battles of the Civil War, and it was a tactical Confederate victory. While the Army of the Potomac's I and XI Corps engaged in heavy fighting, they were eventually flanked from the north by Ewell's Corps, which was returning toward Gettysburg from its previous objective. After a disorderly retreat through the town itself, the Union men began to dig in on high ground to the southeast of the town.

It was at this point that Lee arrived on the field and saw the importance of this position. He sent discretionary orders to Ewell that Cemetery Hill be taken "if practicable." Ewell chose not to attempt the assault. Lee's order has been criticized because it left too much discretion to Ewell, leaving historians to speculate on how the more aggressive Stonewall Jackson would have acted on this order if he had lived to command this wing of Lee's army, and how differently the second day of battle would have proceeded with Confederate possession of Culp's Hill or Cemetery Hill. Discretionary orders were customary for General Lee because Jackson and Longstreet, his other principal subordinate, usually reacted to them aggressively and used their initiative to act quickly and forcefully. Ewell's decision not to attack, whether justified or not, may have ultimately cost the Confederates the battle.

General Ewell

With so many men engaged and now taking refuge on the high ground, Meade, who was an engineer like Lee, abandoned his previous plan to draw up a defensive line around Emmittsburg a few miles to the South. After a council of war, the Army of the Potomac determined to defend at Gettysburg.

Day 2

July 2, 1863, Day 2 of the Battle of Gettysburg, may have been the most important day of James Longstreet's career, and it is certainly the most important day of James Longstreet's legacy. The actions of Longstreet's corps that day have affected all the post-war charges, defenses, and historians' opinions about Longstreet ever since.

On the morning of Day 2, Lee decided to attempt attacks on both Union flanks, ordering Ewell's corps to attack Culp's Hill on the Union right while Longstreet's corps would attack on the Union left.

As it turned out, both attacks would come too late. Though there was a controversy over when Lee ordered Longstreet's attack, Longstreet's march got tangled up and caused several hours of delay. Lost Cause advocates attacking Longstreet would later claim his attack was supposed to take place as early as possible, although no official Confederate orders gave a time for the attack. Lee gave the order for the attack around 11:00 a.m., and it is known that Longstreet was reluctant about making it; he still wanted to slide around the Union flank, interpose the Confederate army between Washington D.C. and the Army of the Potomac, and force Meade to attack them. Between Longstreet's delays and the mixup in the march that forced parts of his corps to double back and make a winding march, Longstreet's men weren't ready to attack until about 4:00 p.m.

Longstreet's biographer, Jeffrey Wert, wrote, "Longstreet deserves censure for his performance on the morning of July 2. He allowed his disagreement with Lee's decision to affect his conduct. Once the commanding general determined to assail the enemy, duty required Longstreet to comply with the vigor and thoroughness that had previously characterized his generalship. The concern for detail, the regard for timely information, and the need for preparation were absent." Edwin Coddington, whose history of the Gettysburg Campaign still continues to be considered the best ever written, described Longstreet's march as "a comedy of errors such as one might expect of inexperienced commanders and raw militia, but not of Lee's ' War Horse' and his veteran troops." Coddington considered it "a dark moment in Longstreet's career as a general."

Writing about Day 2, Longstreet criticized Lee, insisting once again that the right move was to move around the Union flank. "The opportunity for our right was in the air. General Halleck saw it from Washington. General Meade saw and was apprehensive of it. Even General Pendleton refers to it in favorable mention in his official report. Failing to adopt it, General Lee should have gone with us to his right. He had seen and carefully examined the left of his line, and only gave us a guide to show the way to the right, leaving the battle to be adjusted to formidable and difficult grounds without his assistance. If he had been with us, General Hood's messengers could have been referred to general Headquarters, but to delay and send messengers five miles in favor of a move that he had rejected would have been contumacious. The opportunity was with the Confederates from the assembling on Cemetery Hill. It was inviting of their preconceived plans. It was the object of and excuse for the invasion as a substitute for more direct efforts for the relief of Vicksburg. Confederate writers and talkers claim that General Meade could have escaped without making aggressive battle, but that is equivalent to confession of the inertia that failed to grasp the opportunity."

The delay would ultimately allow the Army of the Potomac to move men onto Little Round Top, high ground that commanded much of the field. Though there were delays in his corps' movement, Longstreet's men delivered a ferocious attack. Longstreet's and Hill's men smashed the Union soldiers, particularly the III Corps, which commander Dan Sickles had moved forward nearly a mile against Meade's orders. The salient in the Union army's line led to much of the effort of the attack taking place there, and the North was able to hold off the attacks against Little Round Top.

Meanwhile, Ewell's attack against Culp's Hill on the other end of the field met with some success in pushing the Army of the Potomac back. However, the attack started so late in the day that nightfall made it impossible for the Confederates to capitalize on their success. Ewell's men would spend the night at the base of Culp's Hill and partially up the hill, but it would fall upon them to pick up the attack the next morning.

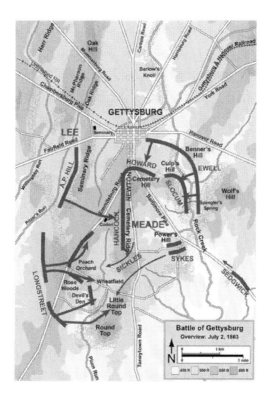

That night, Meade held another council of war. Having been attacked on both flanks, Meade and his top officers correctly surmised that Lee would attempt an attack on the center of the line the next day. Moreover, captured Confederates and the fighting and intelligence of Day 2 let it be known that the only Confederate unit that had not yet seen action during the fighting was George Pickett's division of Longstreet's corps.

General Meade

Day 3

After the attack on Day 2, Longstreet spent the night continuing to plot potential movements around Little Round Top and Big Round Top, thinking that would again get the Confederate army around the Union's flank. Longstreet himself did not realize that a reserve corps of the Union army was poised to block that maneuver.

Longstreet did not meet with Lee on the night of July 2, so when Lee met with him the following morning he found Longstreet's men were not ready to conduct an early morning attack, which Lee had wanted to attempt just as he was on the other side of the lines against Culp's Hill. With Pickett's men not up, however, Longstreet's corps couldn't make such an attack. Lee later wrote that Longstreet's "dispositions were not completed as early as was expected."

On the morning of July 3, the Confederate attack against Culp's Hill fizzled out, but by then Lee had already planned a massive attack on the Union center, combined with having Stuart's cavalry attack the Union army's lines in the rear. A successful attack would split the Army of the Potomac at the same time its communication and supply lines were severed by Stuart, which would make it possible to capture the entire army in detail.

There was just one problem with the plan, as Longstreet told Lee that morning: no 15,000 men who ever existed could successfully execute the attack. The charge required marching across an open field for about a mile, with the Union artillery holding high ground on all sides of the incoming Confederates. Longstreet ardently opposed the attack, but, already two days into the battle, Lee explained that because the Army of the Potomac was here on the field, he must strike at it. Longstreet later wrote that he said, "General Lee, I have been a soldier all my life. It is my opinion that no fifteen thousand men ever arrayed for battle can take that position."[9] Longstreet proposed instead that their men should slip around the Union forces and occupy the high ground, forcing Northern commanders to attack them, rather than *vice versa*.

Realizing the insanity of sending 15,000 men hurtling into all the Union artillery, Lee planned to use the Confederate artillery to try to knock out the Union artillery ahead of time. Although old friend William Pendleton was the artillery chief, the artillery cannonade would be supervised by Edward Porter Alexander, Longstreet's chief artillerist, who would have to give the go-ahead to the charging infantry because they were falling under Longstreet's command. Alexander later noted that Longstreet was so disturbed and dejected about ordering the attack that at one point he tried to make Alexander order the infantry forward, essentially doing Longstreet's dirty work for him.

As Longstreet had predicted, from the beginning the plan was an abject failure. Stuart's men did not defeat the Union cavalry and thus had no success. Just after 1:00 p.m. 150 Confederate guns began to fire from Seminary Ridge, hoping to incapacitate the Union center before launching an infantry attack, but they mostly overshot their mark. The artillery duel could be heard from dozens of miles away, and all the smoke led to Confederate artillery constantly overshooting their targets. Eventually, Union artillery chief Henry Hunt cleverly figured that if the Union cannons stopped firing back, the Confederates might think they successfully knocked out the Union batteries. On top of that, the Union would be preserving its ammunition for the impending charge that everyone now knew was coming. When they stopped, Lee, Alexander, and others mistakenly concluded that they'd knocked out the Union artillery.

A short time later, Confederate General George Pickett, commander of one of the three divisions under General Longstreet, prepared for the *Lee-designed* charge (henceforth known as "Pickett's Charge") aimed at the Union center. With his men in position, Pickett asked Longstreet to give the order to advance, but Longstreet would only nod, fearing that "to verbalize the order may reveal his utter lack of confidence in the plan." And while most of the men participating in that charge had been led to believe that the battle was nearly over and that all that remained was to march unopposed to Cemetery Hill, in actually, those men were unwittingly walking into a virtual massacre.

As the Confederate line advanced, Union cannon on Cemetery Ridge and Little Round Top began blasting away, with Confederate soldiers continuing to march forward. One Union soldier

---

[9]   Gaffney, P. and D. Gaffney. *The Civil War: Exploring History One Week at a Time*. Page 282.

later wrote, "We could not help hitting them with every shot . . . a dozen men might be felled by one single bursting shell."[10] By the time Longstreet's men reached Emmitsburg Road, Union artillery switched to firing canister (tin cans filled with iron and lead balls), and as the Confederate troops continued to approach the Union center, Union troops positioned behind the wall cut down the oncoming Confederates, easily decimating both flanks. And while some of the men did mange to advance to the Union line and engage in hand-to-hand combat, it was of little consequence.

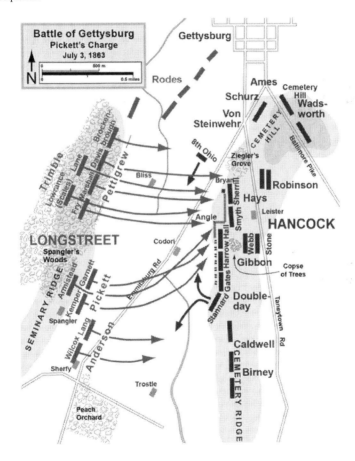

10   Gaffney, P. and D. Gaffney. *The Civil War: Exploring History One Week at a Time*. Page 283.

In about an hour, nearly 6,500 Confederates were dead or wounded, five times that of the Union, with all 13 regimental commanders in Pickett's division killed or wounded. In the aftermath of the defeat, General Longstreet stated, "General Lee came up as our troops were falling back and encouraged them as well as he could; begged them to reform their ranks and reorganize their forces . . . and it was then he used the expression . . . 'It was all my fault; get together, and let us do the best we can toward saving which is left to us.'"[11] Longstreet never resisted an opportunity to distance himself from failure and direct it towards someone else, even Lee.

Today Pickett's Charge is remembered as the American version of the Charge of the Light Brigade, a heroic but completely futile march that had no chance of success. In fact, it's remembered as Pickett's Charge because Pickett's Virginians wanted to claim the glory of getting the furthest during the attack in the years after the war. The charge consisted of about 15,000 men under the command of James Longstreet, with three divisions spearheaded by Pickett, Trimble, and Pettigrew. Trimble and Pettigrew were leading men from A.P. Hill's corps, and Hill was too disabled by illness that day to choose the men from his corps to make the charge. As a result, some of the men who charged that day had already engaged in heavy fighting.

Longstreet was so sure of disaster that he could barely take it upon himself to order the men ahead. He was right. The charge suffered about a 50% casualty rate, as the Confederates marched into hell. The men barely made a dent in the Union line before retreating in disorder back across the field, where Lee met them in an effort to regroup them in case the Union counterattacked. At one point, Lee ordered Pickett to reform his division, to which Pickett reportedly cried, "I have no division!"

---

[11] Davis, Kenneth C. *The Civil War: Everything You Need to Know About America's Greatest Conflict but Never Learned*. Page 306.

Pickett

After the South had lost the war, the importance of Gettysburg as one of the "high tide" marks of the Confederacy became apparent to everyone, making the battle all the more important in the years after it had been fought. Former Confederate comrades like Longstreet and Jubal Early would go on to argue who was responsible for the loss at Gettysburg (and thus the war) in the following decades. Much of the debate was fueled by those who wanted to protect Lee's legacy, especially because Lee was dead and could not defend himself in writing anymore. However, on July 3, Lee insisted on taking full blame for what occurred at Gettysburg, telling his retreating men, "It's all my fault." Historians have mostly agreed, placing the blame for the disastrous Day 3 on Lee's shoulders. Porter Alexander would later call it Lee's "worst day" of the war.

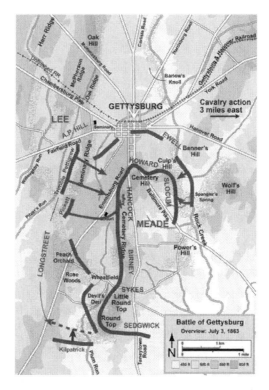

Although it was not immediately apparent where the blame rested for such a devastating loss, not long after the Battle of Gettysburg two names kept surfacing: cavalry leader General "Jeb" Stuart and General James Longstreet; Stuart blamed for robbing Lee of the "eyes" he needed to know of Union movement, and Longstreet for delaying his attack on Round Top Hills the second day and acting too slowly in executing the assault on the Union left flank.

Coincidentally, Gettysburg was the second battle in which Longstreet was incorrectly reported killed. On Saturday, July 4, the *Washington Star* reported that prisoners of the final battle "assert that [in addition to Confederate General William] Barksdale, Longstreet was also killed."[12] On Monday, July 6, the *Star* reported, "Longstreet was mortally wounded and captured. He is reported to have died an hour afterward."[13] Yet again, these reports were incorrect.

---

[12]   Stepp, John, W. and Hill, William I. (editors). *Mirror of War, The Washington Star Reports the Civil War.* Page 203.
[13]   Stepp, John, W. and Hill, William I. (editors). *Mirror of War, The Washington Star Reports the Civil War.* Page 206.

Chickamauga

In June of 1863, Union general William Rosecrans marched southeast toward Chattanooga, Tennessee, in pursuit of Confederate general Braxton Bragg, intending to "drive him into the sea." By this point, both the Union and Confederates had realized how uniquely important Chattanooga was as the rail and road gateway to all points south of the Ohio River and east of the Mississippi River.

In mid-September, the Union Army under General Rosecrans had taken Chattanooga, but rather than be pushed out of the action, Bragg decided to stop with his 60,000 men and prepare a counterattack south of Chattanooga at a creek named Chickamauga. To bolster his fire-power, Confederate President Jefferson Davis sent 12,000 additional troops (some sources say as many as 60,000) under the command of Lieutenant General Longstreet. In only nine days, Longstreet had successfully moved his entire corps by rail to come to Bragg's aid.

On the morning of September 19, 1863, Bragg's men assaulted the Union line, which was established in a wooded area thick with underbrush along the river. That day and the morning of the next, Bragg continue to pummel Union forces, with the battle devolving from an organized succession of coordinated assaults into what one Union soldier described as "a mad, irregular battle, very much resembling guerilla warfare on a vast scale in which one army was bushwhacking the other, and wherein all the science and the art of war went for nothing."[14]

Late that second morning, Rosecrans was misinformed that a gap was forming in his front line, so he responded by moving several units forward to shore it up. What Rosecrans didn't realize, however, was that in doing so he accidentally created a quarter-mile gap in the Union center, directly in the path of an eight-brigade (15,000 man) force led by Longstreet. Described by one of Rosecrans' own men as "an angry flood," Longstreet's attack, which historians are split on whether it was skill or luck, was successful in driving one-third of the Union Army to the crossroads of Rossville, five miles north, with Rosecrans himself running all the way to Chattanooga where he was later found weeping and seeking solace from a staff priest.

The destruction of the entire army was prevented by General George H. Thomas, who rallied the remaining parts of the army and formed a defensive stand on Horseshoe Ridge. Union units spontaneously rallied to create a defensive line on their fall-back point at Horseshoe Ridge-- forming a new right wing for the line of Maj. General George H. Thomas, who had now assumed overall command of the remaining forces. And although the Confederates launched a series of well-executed (albeit costly) assaults, Thomas and his men managed to hold until nightfall, when they made an orderly retreat to Chattanooga while the Confederates occupied the surrounding

---

[14]   Gaffney, P. and D. Gaffney. *The Civil War: Exploring History One Week at a Time.* Page 305.

heights, ultimately besieging the city. Dubbed "The Rock of Chickamauga", Thomas's heroics ensured that Rosecrans' army was able to successfully retreat back to Chattanooga.

In the aftermath of the Battle of Chickamauga, Longstreet blamed the number of men lost during what would be the bloodiest battle of the Western Theater on Bragg's incompetence, also criticizing him for refusing to pursue the escaping Union army. He later stated to Jefferson Davis, "Nothing but the hand of God can help as long as we have our present commander."[15] Bragg owed his position to being a close friend of Jefferson Davis's, and one of the criticisms often lodged at Davis by historians is that he played favorites to the detriment of the South's chances. Even after he reluctantly removed Bragg from command out West, he would bring Bragg to Richmond to serve as a military advisor.

Bragg

Following the victory at Chickamauga, Longstreet departed on an independent mission to expel the Union army from Knoxville, Tennessee--operations that would fail due to what Longstreet explained away as "weakened forces and disagreeable subordinates." Longstreet then took a position at Gordonsville, Virginia where he was poised to protect against Union invasion via the Shenandoah Valley, or quickly reunite with the main body of Lee's Army of Northern Virginia should the main thrust of Union movement advance towards Fredericksburg. On May 4, 1864, upon finding out that his long-time friend General Ulysses S. Grant was now in command of the Union Army, Longstreet confided to his fellow officers, "He will fight us every day and every hour until the end of the war."[16]

---

[15]   Gaffney, P. and D. Gaffney. *The Civil War: Exploring History One Week at a Time*. Page 306.

Battle of the Wilderness

Although the Army of the Potomac had been victorious at Gettysburg, Lincoln was still upset at what he perceived to be General George Meade's failure to trap Robert E. Lee's Army of Northern Virginia in Pennsylvania. When Lee retreated from Pennsylvania without much fight from the Army of the Potomac, Lincoln was again discouraged, believing Meade had a chance to end the war if he had been bolder. Though historians dispute that, and the Confederates actually invited attack during their retreat, Lincoln was constantly looking for more aggressive fighters to lead his men.

With Lee continuing to hold off the Army of the Potomac in a stalemate along the same battle lines at the end of 1863, Lincoln shook things up. In March 1864, Grant was promoted to lieutenant general and given command of all the armies of the United States. His first acts of command were to keep General Halleck in position to serve as a liaison between Lincoln and Secretary of War Edwin Stanton. And though it's mostly forgotten today, Grant technically kept General Meade in command of the Army of the Potomac, even though Grant attached himself to that army before the Overland Campaign in 1864 and thus served as its commander for all intents and purposes.

In May 1864, with Grant now attached to the Army of the Potomac, the Civil War's two most famous generals met each other on the battlefield for the first time. Lee had won stunning victories at battles like Chancellorsville and Second Bull Run by going on the offensive and taking the strategic initiative, but Grant and Lincoln had no intention of letting him do so anymore. Grant ordered General Meade, "Lee's army is your objective point. Wherever Lee goes, there you will go also."

By 1864, things were looking so bleak for the South that the Confederate war strategy was simply to ensure Lincoln lost reelection that November, with the hope that a new Democratic president would end the war and recognize the South's independence. With that, and given the shortage in manpower, Lee's strategic objective was to continue defending Richmond, while hoping that Grant would commit some blunder that would allow him a chance to seize an opportunity.

On May 4, 1864, Grant launched the Overland Campaign, crossing the Rapidan River near Fredericksburg with the 100,000 strong Army of the Potomac, which almost doubled Lee's hardened but battered Army of Northern Virginia. It was a similar position to the one George McClellan had in 1862 and Joe Hooker had in 1863, and Grant's first attack, at the Battle of the

---

[16]   Rhea, Gordon C. *The Battle of the Wilderness May 5–6, 1864.* Page 42.

Wilderness, followed a similar pattern. Nevertheless, Lee proved more than capable on the defensive.

From May 5-6, Lee's men won a tactical victory at the Battle of the Wilderness, which was fought so close to where the Battle of Chancellorsville took place a year earlier that soldiers encountered skeletons that had been buried in (too) shallow graves in 1863. Both armies sustained heavy casualties while Grant kept attempting to move the fighting to a setting more to his advantage, but the heavy forest made coordinated movements almost impossible.

On the second day, the aggressive Lee used General Longstreet's corps to counterattack on the second day. In his first confrontation since rejoining Lee's army, Longstreet launched a powerful flanking attack along the Orange Plank Road against the Union II Corps and nearly drove it off the field. Then instituting what are recognized as innovative tactics to deal with difficult terrain, Longstreet ordered the advance of six brigades by heavy skirmish lines--four to flank the Union right and two against the front--which allowed his men to deliver continuous fire into the enemy while proving elusive targets themselves.

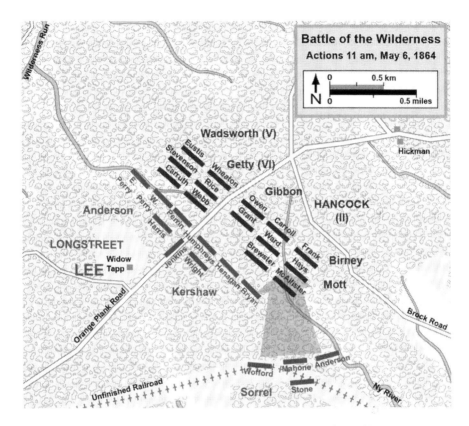

Battle of the Wilderness
Actions 11 am, May 6, 1864

Almost exactly a year earlier, just miles away from where the Battle of the Wilderness was fought, Stonewall Jackson was mortally wounded by fire from his own men. Longstreet nearly suffered the same fate. During the assault, Longstreet was himself wounded — accidentally shot by one of his own men – with the ball passing through the base of his neck and lodging in his shoulder. To assure his men, Longstreet raised his hat as he was being carried off the field, but with Longstreet incapacitated, the momentum of the attack was lost, forcing General Lee to delay further action until units could be realigned. This setback gave Union defenders sufficient time to reorganize.

By the end of the day, the battle ended at virtually the same place it had started that morning-- except that now, thousands of men lied dead. Confederate General Edward Porter Alexander later spoke of the loss of Longstreet at the critical juncture of the battle, saying, "I have always believed that, but for Longstreet's fall, the panic which was fairly underway in Hancock's Corps would have been extended and have resulted in Grant's being forced to retreat back across the

Rapidan."[17]

The Rest of the Overland Campaign

Longstreet was forced to rest and convalesce during the rest of the Overland Campaign. Grant disengaged from the battle in the same position was Hooker before him at Chancellorsville, McClellan on the Virginian Peninsula, and Burnside after Fredericksburg. His men got the familiar dreadful feeling that they would retreat back across the Rapidan toward Washington, as they had too many times before. This time, however, Grant made the fateful decision to keep moving south, inspiring his men by telling them that he was prepared to "fight it out on this line if it takes all Summer."[18]

Using the Union V Corps under Major General Gouverneur K. Warren, Grant moved forward in a series of flanking maneuvers that continued to move the army steadily closer to Richmond. But Lee continued to parry each thrust. The next major battle took place at Spotsylvania Court House from May 8-21, with the heaviest fighting on May 12 when a salient in the Confederate line nearly spelled disaster. Fighting raged around the "Bloody Angle" for hours, with soldiers fighting hand to hand before the Confederates finally dislodged the Union soldiers."

---

[17]   Alexander, Edward P. (Gallagher, Gary W. editor). *Fighting for the Confederacy: The Personal Recollections of General Edward Porter Alexander.* Page 360.
[18]   Fellman, Michael. *The Making of Robert E. Lee.* Page 167.

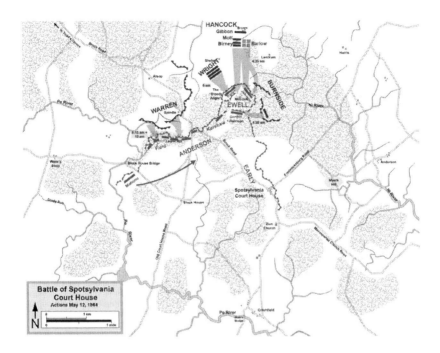

Lee's army continued to stoutly defend against several attacks by the Army of the Potomac, but massive casualties were inflicted on both sides. After Spotsylvania, Grant had already incurred about 35,000 casualties while inflicting nearly 25,000 casualties on Lee's army. Grant, of course, had the advantage of a steady supply of manpower, so he could afford to fight the war of attrition. It was a fact greatly lost on the people of the North, however, who knew Grant's track record from Shiloh and saw massive casualty numbers during the Overland Campaign. Grant was routinely criticized as a butcher.

As fate would have it, the only time during the Overland Campaign Lee had a chance to take the initiative was after Spotsylvania. During the fighting that came to be known as the Battle of North Anna, Lee was heavily debilitated with illness. Grant nearly fell into Lee's trap by splitting his army in two along the North Anna before avoiding it.

By the time the two armies reached Cold Harbor near the end of May 1864, Grant incorrectly thought that Lee's army was on the verge of collapse. Though his frontal assaults had failed spectacularly at places like Vicksburg, Grant believed that Lee's army was on the ropes and could be knocked out with a strong attack. The problem was that Lee's men were now masterful at quickly constructing defensive fortifications, including earthworks and trenches, that made their positions impregnable. While Civil War generals kept employing Napoleonic tactics, Civil War soldiers were building the types of defensive works that would be the harbinger of World War I's trench warfare.

At Cold Harbor, Grant decided to order a massive frontal assault against Lee's well fortified and entrenched lines. His decision was dead wrong, literally. Although the story of Union soldiers pinning their names on the back of their uniforms in anticipation of death at Cold Harbor is apocryphal, the frontal assault on June 3 inflicted thousands of Union casualties in about half an hour. With another 12,000 casualties at Cold Harbor, Grant had suffered about as many casualties in a month as Lee had in his entire army at the start of the campaign. Grant later admitted, ""I have always regretted that the last assault at Cold Harbor was ever made...No advantage whatever was gained to compensate for the heavy loss we sustained."

Although Grant's results were widely condemned, he continued to push toward Richmond. After Cold Harbor, Grant managed to successfully steal an entire day's march on Lee and crossed the James River, attacking the Confederacy's primary railroad hub at Petersburg, which was only a few miles from Richmond. By the time Lee's army reached Petersburg, it had been defended by P.G.T. Beauregard, but now the Army of Northern Virginia had been pinned down at Petersburg. The two armies dug in, and Grant prepared for a long term siege of the vital city.

Petersburg

Although he'd lost the use of his right arm and could not speak above a whisper, in October of 1864, Longstreet reassumed command of his corps and joined Lee's forces at Petersburg, Virginia. At Cedar Creek on October 19, Union General Philip Sheridan executed a stunning victory over Longstreet, capturing 43 pieces of Confederate artillery and taking numerous prisoners--including Confederate general Stephan Dodson.

Grant had not won a single victory during the Overland Campaign, and though his strategic objective of attacking Lee and taking Richmond was still in the process of being accomplished, Grant's results certainly weren't helping Lincoln's reelection prospects, with Democrats hammering him for the staggering costliness of the war. Instead, it would be the scourge of the South who saved the day. With Grant in the East, control of the Western theater was turned over to William Tecumseh Sherman, who beat back Joseph E. Johnston and John Bell Hood in the Atlanta campaign, taking the important Southern city in early September. On September 3, 1864, Sherman telegrammed Lincoln, "Atlanta is ours and fairly won." So was Lincoln's reelection two months later.

While Sherman took Atlanta and began his famous "March to the Sea", Grant and Lee continued to hunker down at Petersburg, with the Army of the Potomac gradually expanding the siege lines and moving them closer in an attempt to fatally stretch Lee's defenses. While Grant held Lee and his armies in check, Sherman's army cut through Georgia and cavalry forces led by General Phillip H. Sheridan destroyed railroads and supplies in Northern Virginia, particularly in the Shenandoah Valley. Lee had almost no initiative, at one point futilely sending General Jubal Early with a contingent through the Shenandoah Valley and toward Washington D.C. in an effort to peel off some of Grant's men. Though Early made it to the outskirts of Washington D.C. and Lincoln famously became the only president to come under enemy fire at Fort Stevens, the Union's "Little Phil" Sheridan pushed Early back through the Valley and scorched it.

Sheridan

The siege would carry on for nearly 10 months, and during the siege the famous battle during took place when Union engineers burrowed underneath the Confederate siege lines and lit the fuse on a massive amount of ammunition, creating a "crater" in the field. But even then, the Battle of the Crater ended with a Union debacle, as Union forces swarmed into the crater instead of around it, giving the Confederates the ability to practically shoot fish in a barrel.

Still, by the beginning of 1865, the Confederacy was in utter disarray. The main Confederate army in the West under John Bell Hood had been nearly destroyed by General Thomas's men at the Battle of Franklin in late 1864, and Sherman's army faced little resistance as it marched through the Carolinas. Although Confederate leaders remained optimistic, by the summer of 1864 they had begun to consider desperate measures in an effort to turn around the war. From 1863-1865, Confederate leaders had even debated whether to conscript black slaves and enlist them as soldiers. Even as their fortunes looked bleak, the Confederates refused to issue an official policy to enlist blacks. It was likely too late to save the Confederacy anyway.

By the time Lincoln delivered his Second Inaugural Address in March 1865, the end of the war was in sight. That month, Lincoln famously met with Grant, Sherman, and Admiral David Porter at City Point, Grant's headquarters during the siege, to discuss how to handle the end of the war.

George P.A. Healy's famous 1868 painting, "The Peacemakers", depicts the meeting at City Point

Lee's siege lines at Petersburg were finally broken on April 1 at the Battle of Five Forks, which is best remembered for General George Pickett (best remembered for Pickett's Charge) enjoying a cod bake lunch while his men were being defeated. Historians have attributed it to unusual environmental acoustics that prevented Pickett and his staff from hearing the battle despite their close proximity, not that it mattered to the Confederates at the time. Between that and Gettysburg, Pickett and Lee were alleged to have held very poor opinions of each other by the end of the war, and there is still debate as to whether Lee had ordered Pickett out of the army during the Appomattox campaign. The following day, battles raged across the siege lines of Petersburg, eventually spelling the doom for Lee's defenses. On April 2, 1865, Lee abandoned Petersburg, and thus Richmond with it.

Appomattox

Withdrawing from Petersburg with Lee, Longstreet then led his troops towards Appomattox.

Lee's battered army began stumbling toward a rail depot in the hopes of avoiding being surrounded by Union forces and picking up much needed food rations. While Grant's army continued to chase Lee's retreating army westward, the Confederate government sought to escape across the Deep South. On April 4, President Lincoln entered Richmond and toured the home of Confederate President Jefferson Davis.

Fittingly, the food rations did not arrive as anticipated. On April 7, 1865, Grant sent Lee the first official letter demanding Lee's surrender. In it Grant wrote, "The results of the last week must convince you of the hopelessness of further resistance on the part of the Army of Northern Virginia in this struggle. I feel it is so, and regret it as my duty to shift myself from the responsibility of any further effusion of blood by asking of you the surrender of that portion of the Confederate States army known as the Army of Northern Virginia."[19] Passing the note to General Longstreet, now his only advisor, Longstreet said, "Not yet."[20] But by the following evening during what would be the final Confederate Council of War (and after one final attempt had been made to break through Union lines), Lee finally succumbed, stating regretfully, "There is nothing left me but to go and see General Grant, and I had rather die a thousand deaths."[21]

Communications continued until April 9, at which point Lee and Grant two met at Appomattox Court House. When Lee and Grant met, the styles in dress captured the personality differences perfectly. Lee was in full military attire, while Grant showed up casually in a muddy uniform. The Civil War's two most celebrated generals were meeting for the first time since the Mexican-American War.

---

[19]   Horn, Stanley F. (editor). *The Robert E. Lee Reader.* Page 436.
[20]   Davis, Kenneth C. *The Civil War: Everything You Need to Know About America's Greatest Conflict but Never Learned.* Page 402.
[21]   Davis, Kenneth C. *The Civil War: Everything You Need to Know About America's Greatest Conflict but Never Learned.* Page 402.

The McLean Parlor in Appomattox Court House. McLean's house was famously fought around during the First Battle of Bull Run, leading him to move to Appomattox.

The Confederate soldiers had continued fighting while Lee worked out the terms of surrender, and they were understandably devastated to learn that they had surrendered. Some of his men had famously suggested to Lee that they continue to fight on. Porter Alexander would later rue the fact that he suggested to Lee that they engage in guerrilla warfare, which earned him a stern rebuke from Lee. As a choked-up Lee rode down the troop line on his famous horse Traveller that day, he addressed his defeated army, saying, "Men, we have fought through the war together. I have done my best for you; my heart is too full to say more."

Appomattox is frequently cited as the end of the Civil War, but there still remained several Confederate armies across the country, mostly under the command of General Joseph E. Johnston, who Lee had replaced nearly 3 years earlier. On April 26, Johnston surrendered all of his forces to General Sherman. Over the next month, the remaining Confederate forces would surrender or quit. The last skirmish between the two sides took place May 12-13, ending ironically with a Confederate victory at the Battle of Palmito Ranch in Texas. Two days earlier, Jefferson Davis had been captured in Georgia.

Although the surrender of the Army of Northern Virginia to General Ulysses S. Grant and the Army of the Potomac at Appomattox Courthouse did not officially end the long and bloody Civil War, the surrender is often considered the final chapter of the war. For that reason, Appomattox has captured the popular imagination of Americans ever since Lee's surrender there on April 9, 1865.

Chapter 8: The Post-War Years, 1865-1904

Military Life, Final years

Shortly after the end of the Civil War, James Longstreet was appointed the Adjutant General of the Louisiana State Militia by the Republican Governor of that state, and by 1872 became Major General in command of all New Orleans militia and state police forces.

In 1874, one of his most controversial post-War incidents occurred during protests of election irregularities, when an armed force of 8,400 "White League" members advanced on the State House. Longstreet, in command of a 3,600 man force comprised of Metropolitan Police, city police, and African-American militia troops armed with two Gatling guns and a battery of artillery, foolishly rode into the crowd of protesters and was promptly pulled from his horse, shot, and taken prisoner. Emboldened by his capture, the 'White League' then charged, causing many of Longstreet's men to flee or surrender, with 38 men ultimately killed and 79 wounded, prompting Federal troops to be called in to restore order.

Longstreet's use of Black troops during this disturbance increased his denunciations by anti-Reconstructionists.

Personal Life, Final Years

Longstreet in later years

During the post-War Reconstruction, Longstreet fell drastically out of public favor. His political attitudes, criticism of Lee at Gettysburg (who Longstreet referred to as "Marse Robert," a term of endearment reserved for friends), and outspoken admiration for Radical Republican and former Union commander Ulysses S. Grant (who became the 18th President of the United States in 1869) only amplified the ire and resentment of the Southern people.

Moving to New Orleans, Longstreet took a position as an insurance company president but was soon ousted. Having joined the Republican Party, "Lincoln's Party", directly after the War, he found that all his employment (and personal) opportunities were limited to Republican prospects, which dried up after the Democrats assumed control. Thus he was forced to accept positions as postmaster, U. S. Marshall, and in 1880, Ambassador to Turkey (an appointment provided by President Grant). Then from 1896 (or 1898) until his death in 1904, he served as U. S. Commissioner of Railroads.

In June of 1867, Longstreet was asked by a reporter from a local newspaper how Louisiana should respond to the new Federal mandate that required former Confederate states to give Blacks the vote. Longstreet responded that the South should obey; that *might makes right*. "The ideas that divided political parties before the war, upon the rights of the States, were thoroughly discussed by our wisest statesmen, and eventually appealed to the arbitrament of the sword. The decision was in favor of the North . . . and should be accepted."[22] Longstreet was immediately denounced as a traitor by many Southerners; some speculating that he had been a traitor all along. In his 1896 memoirs, he wrote that the day after he made that statement, "old comrades passed me on the streets without speaking."

In 1884, Longstreet relocated to Gainesville, Georgia, where he went into semi-retirement on a 65 acre farm his neighbors referred to mockingly as "Gettysburg," where he raised turkeys, grew orchards, and set up vineyards on terraced ground, all while writing his memoirs.

Loss, Death, Remarriage, Resolve

On April 9, 1889 (the 24th anniversary of Lee's surrender at Appomattox), a devastating fire occurred (which many saw simply as *come-uppance*) that destroyed Longstreet's house and most of his personal possessions, including his personal Civil War documents and memorabilia (which partly explains why so little written about his youth still exists). Then in December of that year, Maria Louise Garland, his wife of 40 years, died.

On September 8, 1897, the 76 year old Longstreet married his second wife, the 34 year old Helen Dortch of Atlanta, Georgia. Although Longstreet's children are said to have reacted poorly to the marriage, by all accounts, Helen was a devoted wife and avid supporter of James' legacy after his death. Helen would outlive James by 58 years, dying in 1962 at the age of 99.

In his final years, the American people, for the most part, seems to have forgotten about the post-War controversies and once again recognized Longstreet as a principal leader during the Civil War; once again recognizing him as the field commander who had once warranted the designation of Lee's "War Horse", even though it was a term he personally despised. He and General George Pickett remained friends to his final days.

Longstreet, Author

In 1896, James Longstreet published his memoirs, *From Manassas to Appomattox*. While considered overtly defensive in tone and containing numerable inconsistencies, contradictions, half-truths, and outright lies, it is nonetheless viewed today as an important source of insight into the Civil War, this portion of American history, and of course, James Longstreet himself.

In Memoriam

On January 2, 1904 at the age of nearly 83, Longstreet died while visiting Gainesville. He was

---

[22]   Gaffney, P. and D. Gaffney. *The Civil War: Exploring History One Week at a Time.* Page 442.

buried in Alta Vista Cemetery, Hall County, Georgia.

An indication of how long it has taken for Longstreet to get the credit he deserved for his participation in the war can be found in the fact that only recently was a monument to Longstreet constructed at Gettysburg. There is no special recognition at Hollywood Cemetery in Richmond, Virginia (although there are for George Pickett and "Jeb" Stuart), and most, if not all, Confederate Generals are buried in Hollywood rather than Gettysburg National Cemetery.

Homage

According to *The Confederate Image: Prints of the Lost Cause*, "There [is] nothing mysterious about the scarcity of portraits of General Longstreet . . . it seems a near-miracle that two survive," (a lithograph by J. L. Giles and an engraving made in France by Goupil et cie.)[23] As this text explains, the production of such prints "was determined by postwar myth as much as wartime performance, and there was good reason to shunt Longstreet aside for other heroes."

While it is true that for a brief period of time after Stonewall Jackson's death, General Longstreet held a command of great importance that *could* have led to assuming Jackson's former status as unequivocal champion of the South -- second only to Robert E. Lee -- immediately following the War, he quickly embraced what he termed "practical reconstruction and reconciliation," stating, "The sword has decided in favor of the North . . . [and Northern principles] cease to be principles and become law."[24] After becoming an avowed Republican and Grant supporter in 1869 (as well as devout Catholic), the vast majority of Southerners shunned him. (It is most likely that the Giles lithograph was made before that date, before he was widely deemed a traitor.)

Chapter 9: Longstreet's Legacy/Epilogue

Criticisms

For decades after his death, Longstreet, who was called "Old Pete" by his troops and "Old War Horse" by Lee, was viewed primarily through his arguments with other Confederate generals, his own analyses, and his memoirs. In sum, he was viewed very unflatteringly. To an extent this continues. As historians have since discovered, once weighted against known historical facts, Longstreet's descriptions not only contain flights of fantasy and self-aggrandizing (as autobiographical accounts are prone to do), they contain gross inaccuracies, distortions, and outright lies. Many of his descriptions of events simply did not, *could* not, have occurred as he states. He exaggerates his combat record, grossly overrates his reputation as a corps leader, and boasts of a level of confidence with Lee that simply did not exist. Thus as is academically

---

[23] Neely, Mark E., Holzer, Harold & Boritt, Gabor S. *The Confederate Image.* Page 201.
[24] Neely, Mark E., Holzer, Harold & Boritt, Gabor S. *The Confederate Image.* Page 201.

prudent in such cases, Longstreet's version of history in the memoirs is largely discounted.

Some continue to assert that Longstreet was too selfish and had too high an opinion of himself. To these people, a cursory evaluation of Longstreet's service record makes it clear that whether or not one holds him responsible for the South's defeat at Gettysburg, his behavior there was not an isolated--or even *out-of-character*--incident. It was, in fact, just another episode in a long pattern of behavior at odds with a man entrusted with the second-highest position in the Confederate Army. Even as early as the Battle of Seven Pines on May 31, 1862, though not a particularly significant battle for Longstreet, he'd already begun to reveal ambitions that far exceeded his limitations. Though initially appearing to be a simple unwillingness to cooperate, the underlying disconnect manifested again at Second Manassas (where he responded dangerously slow and was reluctant to attack), his attempted siege of Suffolk (which weighed heavily against him until Lee and Jackson's victory at Chancellorsville overshadowed his lack of good judgment), and then at Knoxville (where his failure was categorically written off as just "one of the winter of 1863-1864 disasters").

Long before Gettysburg, Longstreet was characterized by his men and commanders as "congenitally resistant to hurry himself,"[25] resistant to change of orders (even from his supreme commander, Lee), and disliked to overextend his men (once bivouacked, he allowed his men to prepare three-days' rations before breaking camp, even when they were supposed to stick to a timetable). In fact, his designation as Lee's "old reliable" appears to have been bestowed by someone who had never actually worked with him or had to rely upon him.

Similarly, Longstreet's clash with A. P. Hill, then Jackson, Hood and Toombs, were indicative of his unwillingness to accept that he was not the center of attention; not the one destined for greatness. And, of course, as the War progressed, Longstreet's propensity to find fault (and start feuds) with Lafayette McLaws (who he tried to have court-martialed), Evander Law (who he tried to have arrested), Charles Field, and ultimately, Lee himself, was highly indicative of the self-possessed illusion Longstreet was living (and fighting) under. While always quick to reprimand any subordinate who questioned his orders, he clearly hesitated to resist orders from his superiors on occasions. In his Gettysburg account, Longstreet had the impudence to blame Lee for "not changing his plans" based on Longstreet's "want of confidence in them."

Was Longstreet an Opportunist?

On the surface, it's easy to assume that Longstreet paid his dues and earned his advancement in the Confederate Army. And in that he was one of the final hold-outs who resisted surrender to the Union until the South was out of options, it's also easy to assume that his loyalty--at least

---

[25]   Dowdey, Clifford. *Lee's Last Campaign: The Story of Lee & His Men against Grant--1864.* Page 134.

during the conflict--was to the Southern cause. But many historians believe that assumption may be ill-conceived.

As a captain in the U. S. Army, Longstreet transferred to the paymaster department in order to achieve a higher rank and pay, that of major, having "denounced all dreams of military glory." Subsequently, (by the majority of accounts), when he enlisted in the Confederate Army, he did not join the troop complement of any particular state--as most soldiers loyal to their state did--he applied directly for the paymaster post, thus securing for himself rank and privilege.

In that Longstreet arrived at Richmond from a New Mexican garrison *via* Texas, arriving later than most officers who came from various army outposts, he *coincidentally* arrived in the War Office at precisely the time a brigadier general was being selected for three regiments of Virginia volunteers. The result of this *coincidence* was that Longstreet started as a brigadier general when most of his peers (some of whom were better experienced) were starting as colonels. This meant that at promotion time, he made major general while they were only making brigadier. Thus, when Lee took control and was forming his two corps, Longstreet's seniority made him next in line for command (alongside "Stonewall" Jackson). But from several military historians' perspectives, he was not the best qualified--just *coincidentally* in the right place at the right time.

Charges of Traitor

After General Robert E. Lee died in October of 1870, a group of ex-Confederates led by General Jubal Early (who had led a division in Ewell's corps at Gettysburg) publicly criticized Longstreet for ignoring orders and delaying his attack on the second day of the Battle on July 2, 1863. But while many former Confederates held Longstreet accountable for not following orders, Early took it one step further, arguing that Longstreet -- not Lee -- was responsible for the Confederate defeat (deemed a "tactical disaster" by most) that by most accounts was the beginning of the end for the Confederacy.

In his memoirs, however, Longstreet defended himself, saying that the blistering post-War attacks concerning Gettysburg were merely "payback for supporting Black suffrage", thus shifting the blame back to Lee. He wrote, "[Lee] knew that I did not believe that success was possible . . . he should have put an officer in charge who had more confidence in his plan."[26] He went on to say that Lee should have given the responsibility to Early, thus justifying his insubordination.

It's also important to note that Lee himself never made any post-War statements to suggest that he held Longstreet responsible for the Confederacy's demise.

A More Positive Perspective

Despite what many considered to be some critical military and personal failures and shortcomings, General James Longstreet is regarded by many today as one of the best, if not *the* best, tactical commanders on either side of the War, even though he did not do well in independent command. Although his emphatic belief that the Confederacy should fight a "strategic offensive-tactical defensive" war was in direct conflict with his commanders (including General Lee), some historians (including Jeffry D. Wert) believe that had Lee followed Longstreet's advice, it is quite likely that not only would the Southern army have endured longer, it possibly would have won the war.

While historians and scholars will continue to disagree on Longstreet's ultimate level of negligence (or incompetence), everyone agrees that he did have a profound effect on the War. And even those who have criticized him have pointed out how thoroughly competent he was

---

[26]   Gaffney, P., and D. Gaffney. *The Civil War: Exploring History One Week at a Time.* Page 442.

when battle was actually joined. Biographer Jeffry Wert wrote "Longstreet ... was the finest corps commander in the Army of Northern Virginia; in fact, he was arguably the best corps commander in the conflict on either side." Richard L. DiNardo wrote, "Even Longstreet's most virulent critics have conceded that he put together the best staff employed by any commander, and that his de facto chief of staff, Lieutenant Colonel G. Moxley Sorrel, was the best staff officer in the Confederacy."

Longstreet's reputation has also been on the upswing in the past few decades, due in no small part to Michael Shaara's 1974 novel *The Killer Angels*, which portrayed Longstreet in a more flattering light. That novel was the basis for the 1993 film *Gettysburg*, which has also helped rehabilitate Longstreet's legacy and helped make clear to the public how instrumental he was during the war. In 1982, Thomas L. Connolly and Barbara L. Bellows published *God and General Longstreet*, which took the Lost Cause proponents like Early to task for their blatant fabrications (such as the one that Lee ordered Longstreet to attack in the early morning of Day 2 of Gettysburg), helping make clear the extent of historical revision propagated by the Lost Cause. In doing so, they cast Longstreet as a sympathetic victim of circumstances and sectional and political hostility.

The Lee Factor

No analysis of Longstreet's contribution to the Civil War would be just or complete without first recognizing the leadership methodology Lee used in guiding his commanders. As many historians point out, in that Lee had not personally trained his field commanders, he was forced to accept these men as they came. Accordingly, Lee's leadership style was designed to promote the individual man's initiative (which most cite as a weakness in his leadership), encouraging them to explore their fullest potential through independent thought.

Thus, Lee did not dictate precise orders (which by his reasoning would have denied each leader's creative participation and sharing of responsibility) but offered what was generally perceived as suggestions or *discretionary* orders. This loose approach to leadership obliged Lee to depend heavily upon each of his field commander's judgment, which, as it turned out, was often in conflict with his own. While some commanders, like "Stonewall" Jackson, urged aggressive and quick movements, others, like Longstreet, preferred defensive tactics. In fact, many historians believe the only reason Longstreet may have blundered during Day 2 of Gettysburg is because Lee gave a discretionary order to a conservative general (Ewell), who refused to take the initiative and attack Culp's Hill on the first night of the battle. Had Jackson survived Chancellorsville and received the same order, he might have made the attack, and if it succeeded there never would have been a 3 day battle at Gettysburg.

For that reason, many military historians contend that as supreme field commander of the Confederate forces, Lee should have adapted his leadership style to best serve the Southern interests, or removed Longstreet at the first sign that he could not be depended upon to follow Lee's lead.

Bibliography

Alexander, Edward P. (Gary W. Gallagher, editor). *Fighting for the Confederacy: The Personal Recollections of General Edward Porter Alexander*. Chapel Hill: University of North Carolina Press, 1989.

Catton, Bruce. *This Hallowed Ground*. New York: Doubleday & Company, Inc., 1956.

Davis, Kenneth C. *The Civil War: Everything You Need to Know About America's Greatest Conflict but Never Learned*. New York: William Morrow and Company, Inc., 1996.

Dowdey, Clifford. *Lee's Last Campaign: The Story of Lee & His Men against Grant--1864*. Lincoln: University of Nebraska Press, 1988.

Gaffney, P., and D. Gaffney. *The Civil War: Exploring History One Week at a Time*. New York: Hyperion, 2011.

Garrison, Webb. *Civil War Curiosities*. Nashville: Rutledge Hill Press, 1994.

Lanning, Michael Lee. *The Civil War 100*. Illinois: Sourcebooks, Inc., 2006.

Neely, Mark E., Holzer, Harold & Boritt, Gabor S. *The Confederate Image*. Chapel Hill: The University of North Carolina Press, 1987.

Phillips, Kevin. *The Cousins' Wars*. New York: Basic Books, 1999.

Rhea, Gordon C. *The Battle of the Wilderness May 5–6, 1864*. Baton Rouge: Louisiana State University Press, 1994.

Sanger, Donald B., & Thomas Robson Hay. *James Longstreet, I: Soldier*. Baton Rouge: Louisiana State University Press, 1952.

Sell, Bill. *Civil War Chronicles: Leaders of the North and South*. New York: MetroBooks, 1996.

Stepp, John, W. and Hill, William I. (editors). *Mirror of War, The Washington Star Reports the Civil War*. The Evening Star Newspaper Co., 1961.

Tagg, Larry. *The Generals of Gettysburg*. CA: Savas Publishing, 1998.

Wert, Jeffry D. *General James Longstreet: The Confederacy's Most Controversial Soldier: A Biography*. New York: Simon & Schuster, 1993.

Printed in Great Britain
by Amazon